To find information on a composition by Bach

To *identify a work* from its genre, title, first words, incipit or BWV number, consult the **BWV** or **Bach Compendium**. There you will find information on the work's date and purpose, scoring, text, sources, transmission, and on facsimiles and notable editions.

For more detailed information on a work's *sources, transmission, and musical text*, consult the **Critical commentary** to the appropriate volume of the **Neue Bach-Ausgabe**.

For *literature* on the work, see its entries in the **BWV** and **Bach Compendium**.

For literature on *Bach's works in the genre*, consult the index of this book, the bibliographies published in the **Bach-Jahrbuch**, and the bibliographies at the beginning of each work group in the **Bach Compendium**.

Abbreviations for important Bach research tools

BC   Hans-Joachim Schulze and Christoph Wolff, *Bach Compendium* [Comprehensive catalogue of Bach's works and their sources]

BG   Bach-Gesellschaft, *Johann Sebastian Bachs Werke* [Complete edition of Bach's music, 1850–1900]

BJ   *Bach-Jahrbuch* [Periodical devoted to Bach studies]

BR   Hans T. David and Arthur Mendel, *The Bach reader* [Translations of many documents of Bach's life]

BWV   Wolfgang Schmieder, *Thematisch-systematisches Verzeichnis der musikalischen Werke von Johann Sebastian Bach: Bach-Werke-Verzeichnis* [Thematic catalogue of Bach's music]

Dok   Bach-Archiv Leipzig, *Bach-Dokumente*, vols. 1–3 [Collected documents of Bach's life]

KB   Kritischer Bericht [Critical commentary volumes accompanying NBA]

NBA   Johann Sebastian Bach, *Neue Ausgabe sämtlicher Werke* [*Neue Bach-Ausgabe:* Complete edition of Bach's music, 1950–]

New Grove   *The New Grove dictionary of music and musicians*, ed. Stanley Sadie

SBB   Staatsbibliothek zu Berlin—Stiftung Preußischer Kulturbesitz [German national library]

An Introduction to Bach Studies

An

Introduction

to Bach Studies

DANIEL R. MELAMED

MICHAEL MARISSEN

NEW YORK • OXFORD

OXFORD UNIVERSITY PRESS

1998

Oxford University Press

Oxford   New York
Athens   Auckland   Bangkok   Bogota   Bombay
Buenos Aires   Calcutta   Cape Town   Dar es Salaam
Delhi   Florence   Hong Kong   Istanbul   Karachi
Kuala Lumpur   Madras   Madrid   Melbourne
Mexico City   Nairobi   Paris   Singapore
Taipei   Tokyo   Toronto   Warsaw

and associated companies in
Berlin   Ibadan

Published by Oxford University Press, Inc.
198 Madison Avenue, New York, New York 10016

Oxford is a registered trademark of Oxford University Press

Library of Congress Cataloging-in-Publication Data
Melamed, Daniel R.
An introduction to Bach studies / Daniel R. Melamed, Michael Marissen.
p. cm.
Includes bibliographical references and index.
ISBN 0-19-512231-3
1. Bach, Johann Sebastian, 1685–1750—Bibliography.
I. Marissen, Michael. II. Title.
ML134.B155M45   1998
016.780'92—dc21   97-40406

1 3 5 7 9 8 6 4 2

Printed in the United States of America
on acid-free paper

Preface

This is a small book about a big subject. The literature on J.S. Bach and his music is enormous, and it should be clear from the outset that we have made no attempt to discuss or even to cite everything published on the composer. Instead, our aim is to bring useful bibliographic resources together in one place, to describe the available tools of Bach research, and to provide starting points for reading on many pieces and topics.

We have provided neither a capsule biography of Bach nor a list of his compositions—the world has enough of these already—but we do give detailed information on where to find them. Most research guides on other composers attempt to present a garland of "all the serious writings" on their subject, but the size of the Bach literature makes this impossible. We have tried instead to mention the principal areas of research for each piece or topic and the most important recent literature.

We have focused on literature that is directly concerned with Bach and Bach studies; there are only a limited number of citations of general works on genres, places, etc., on the assumption that readers will already know where to find them. Similarly, in the section on sources of Bach literature, we have limited our detailed listings to publications concerned principally with Bach, again presuming that readers will know how to find general citations in periodical indexes, collections of dissertation abstracts, and the like.

In citing literature on research topics, on genres, and on individual compositions, we have focused on particularly important writings; on recent literature; on overviews, collections of essays, handbooks, etc.; and on writings in English. In a field that has been around as long as Bach studies, knowing the history of scholarship on a given question is often as important as knowing about the current state of knowledge. In most cases, we have not attempted to outline that history, but rely on the books and articles we cite for that; most good studies begin with a survey of scholarship on their subject.

In several places we offer summaries of particularly important and potentially confusing topics in Bach research: the organization of the annual cantata cycles, pitch standards, the history of the Berlin libraries, the structure of the critical commentary volumes in the Neue Bach-Ausgabe, and so on. We hope that these brief discussions will make the technical literature more understandable.

Most of the volume is aimed at the general scholar and student, but in a few places—especially in the section on sources and transmission—we have presented technical information in greater detail. We hope that having this material collected in one place will be useful to specialists and to those pursuing more advanced work.

For the most part, we have chosen to repeat citations rather than use bibliographic abbreviations or cross references. This takes up more space, but we hope that it will also save flipping around in the book.

In an era in which the nature of musical scholarship is changing particularly fast, it is worth acknowledging that a large proportion of the literature we cite is factual rather than interpretive or critical, and that details of source study and transmission occupy a lot of space here. We do not mean this to be necessarily prescriptive of future research, but merely a reflection of the kind of work that has predominated in Bach studies.

We recognize that our selection of topics and literature does represent a critical judgment about what we believe is important and valuable in Bach research. We have tried to be open-minded, but the idea that a bibliography can be fully objective is a canard, and we accept responsibility for the judgments we have made.

Using this book and getting started in Bach research

1. Get to know the basic tools of Bach research: the BWV, the *Bach Compendium*, the Neue Bach-Ausgabe and its critical commentaries, and the bibliographies of writings on Bach.
2. Consult the inside covers of this book for basic information on getting started in researching a Bach topic.
3. Use the indexes in this book to find topics, authors, and titles. Many subjects are discussed in several different sections of this book, and the indexes will help you find them.

We are grateful to the Yale University Library, Minda Hart from the inter-library loan office at Swarthmore College, to the colleagues who have advised us, especially Gregory Butler, Stephen Crist, George Huber, Robin A. Leaver, and Peter Wollny, and to Reginald L. Sanders for his editorial assistance.

Hamden, Connecticut   D. R. M.
Swarthmore, Pennsylvania   M. M.
February 1997

Contents

To find information on a composition by Bach

To *identify a work* from its genre, title, first words, incipit or BWV number, consult the **BWV** or **Bach Compendium**. There you will find information on the work's date and purpose, scoring, text, sources, transmission, and on facsimiles and notable editions.

For more detailed information on a work's *sources, transmission, and musical text*, consult the **Critical commentary** to the appropriate volume of the **Neue Bach-Ausgabe**.

For *literature* on the work, see its entries in the **BWV** and **Bach Compendium**.

For literature on *Bach's works in the genre*, consult the index of this book, the bibliographies published in the **Bach-Jahrbuch**, and the bibliographies at the beginning of each work group in the **Bach Compendium**.

Abbreviations for important Bach research tools

BC	Hans-Joachim Schulze and Christoph Wolff, *Bach Compendium* [Comprehensive catalogue of Bach's works and their sources]
BG	Bach-Gesellschaft, *Johann Sebastian Bachs Werke* [Complete edition of Bach's music, 1850–1900]
BJ	*Bach-Jahrbuch* [Periodical devoted to Bach studies]
BR	Hans T. David and Arthur Mendel, *The Bach reader* [Translations of many documents of Bach's life]
BWV	Wolfgang Schmieder, *Thematisch-systematisches Verzeichnis der musikalischen Werke von Johann Sebastian Bach: Bach-Werke-Verzeichnis* [Thematic catalogue of Bach's music]
Dok	Bach-Archiv Leipzig, *Bach-Dokumente*, vols. 1–3 [Collected documents of Bach's life]
KB	Kritischer Bericht [Critical commentary volumes accompanying NBA]
NBA	Johann Sebastian Bach, *Neue Ausgabe sämtlicher Werke* [*Neue Bach-Ausgabe:* Complete edition of Bach's music, 1950–]
New Grove	*The New Grove dictionary of music and musicians*, ed. Stanley Sadie
SBB	Staatsbibliothek zu Berlin—Stiftung Preußischer Kulturbesitz [German national library]

An Introduction to Bach Studies

1

Bibliographic tools
of Bach research

In this chapter we present two basic reference tools for Bach research and bibliographies of writings on Bach and his music.

1.1 Basic reference tools

Thematic catalogues have evolved over the years from musically annotated lists of composers' works to comprehensive research tools. There are two for J.S. Bach, and they are the first place to turn for information on the composer's music.

> **Wolfgang Schmieder.** *Thematisch-systematisches Verzeichnis der musik-alischen Werke von Johann Sebastian Bach: Bach-Werke-Verzeichnis (BWV).* **Wiesbaden, 1950, and reprints. 2d ed. 1990.**

Wolfgang Schmieder's *Bach-Werke-Verzeichnis* is the source of the ubiquitous BWV numbers used to identify Bach's compositions. There are two editions, one published in 1950 (actually a reconstruction of materials prepared earlier but destroyed during World War II) and a revision published in 1990. Understanding the organization and limitations of the second edition requires a familiarity with the first, and for reasons discussed below, it is sometimes necessary to consult both.

First edition. In the BWV, there is an entry for each of Bach's works recognized by Schmieder; the main point of access is thus an individual composition. The catalogue is organized by genre. Note that the order of most of the works has nothing to do with the chronology of their composition; for example, the church cantatas are numbered according to the order of their publication in the Bach-Gesellschaft edition. There is an index of first lines of vocal texts, a brief index of names, and a compact index of instrumental themes. The foreword contains important information on lost works not listed in the catalogue, including references to sources no longer available. In light of the drastic revisions in the dating of Bach's works, the

3

chronological listing at the end of the volume is no longer reliable. The three sections of the appendix (Anhang) contain entries for fragmentary and lost works, works of doubtful authenticity, and falsely attributed works, respectively.

One problem with the BWV lies in its treatment of compositions known in multiple versions. The BWV gives strong preference to final versions, listing earlier versions under the same number with a following letter. The revisions listed this way are sometimes minor, but often reflect substantial reworkings with added movements, revised texts, and changed instrumentation for a new occasion. For example, the several versions of the Leipzig-era Reformation Festival cantata "Ein feste Burg ist unser Gott" are collectively listed as BWV 80, and the Weimar-era cantata for Oculi from which several of its movements are taken, "Alles, was von Gott geboren," is listed as BWV 80a, suggesting that this fully independent work is somehow subsidiary to the Leipzig cantata. Some earlier works are subsumed into the listing for their revised versions; for example, there is no entry for Bach's 1733 *Missa* (Kyrie and Gloria) for Dresden, only for this music's later place in the *Mass in B minor* BWV 232.

The entries in the BWV provide the title of each work; its liturgical purpose (where appropriate); information on its text (for vocal works); its scoring (Besetzung); its location in the Bach-Gesellschaft edition; a brief account of the work's origin and history; incipits of each movement or section; information on the work's autograph score if it survives; information on copies (Abschriften), including Bach's original performing parts; individual editions published by Breitkopf & Härtel, the publisher of the BWV (Einzelausgaben B & H); further editions (weitere Ausgaben); and—perhaps most useful—citations to relevant literature (Literatur), including page references in the most important biographies and studies.

Second edition. Nothing as comprehensive as Schmieder's BWV had ever been attempted for Bach's music, and it helped define an era in Bach scholarship. Partly thanks to the BWV, the decade after its publication saw an explosion in Bach research, oriented particularly around the sources for his music and with an emphasis on the genesis and chronology of his works. Much of the information in the BWV thus came in need of revision, not just dates and details of source study, but also the very place of pieces in Bach's output—multiple versions, reconstructed lost works, misattributed compositions, etc.

Though the dates and work histories could easily be revised to reflect current thinking, the structure of the BWV did not lend itself to the incorporation of other kinds of new findings, especially new works and multiple versions of known compositions. What is more, the BWV is the victim of its own success, because its numbering of Bach's works is internationally used. Changing the numbering system must have seemed out of the question— witness the chaos caused by the revisions of Köchel's Mozart catalogue. Added to this is Wolfgang Schmieder's own aversion, discussed in his preface to the second edition, to including reconstructions of lost works as necessarily authentic. As a result, newly identified works and multiple versions of known pieces are handled in less than satisfactory ways in the new edition.

For the most part, the numbering of Bach's works is unchanged. Because of the organization of the first edition, newly discovered works had to be given numbers at the end of the sequence—that is, apart from other works in their genres. They are indicated by sigla that show where in the numbering scheme they belong. For example, the so-called Neumeister chorale preludes are listed as BWV 1090–1120/598→, meaning that their numbers are BWV 1090 to 1120 and that they belong immediately after BWV 598.

Reconstructed works, especially concertos, are given numbers with the suffix R, though they do not consistently receive their own entries.

Works of doubtful authenticity or whose attribution has changed since 1950 are handled in several different ways. Some dubious works remain in the body of the catalogue, for example, the Ouverture in G minor BWV 1070. Others have found new places in the revised appendixes, of which there are now three. Anhang I contains fragmentary and lost works, Anhang II anonymous doubtful works, and Anhang III doubtful works sometimes attributed to J.S. Bach but now ascribed to other composers. (These three appendixes correspond to the three divisions of the appendix in the first edition.) As in the body of the catalogue, new entries in the appendix received new numbers, with their full sigla indicating both their number and where they belong in the original numbering scheme. For example, the serenata "Auf, süß entzückende Gewalt" BWV Anh. 196/Anh. I 14→ was added to the second edition; it received the number Anh. 196 and belongs after the entry Anh. I 14. Many works whose attributions have been revised have moved from one category to another; for example, the formerly anonymous *Magnificat in A minor* now attributed to Melchior Hoffmann carries the new number BWV Anh. I 21/Anh. III 168→, signifying its number (Anh. I 21) and its proper place (after Anh. III 168). We do not know how these new sigla are pronounced.

The information in individual entries has been somewhat reorganized to reflect the significant role of source studies in Bach scholarship. These changes are well explained in the notes at the beginning of the volume. Greatly to the benefit of English-speaking users of the new edition, its rubrics and prefaces are presented both in German and in English. Citations of secondary literature have been brought more up to date, but delays in publishing the second edition meant that despite the 1990 publication date, literature that appeared between approximately 1985 and 1990 is only spottily cited. In addition, many older citations have been deleted, so *to take full advantage of the citations, you must consult both editions of the BWV.*

Hans-Joachim Schulze and Christoph Wolff. *Bach Compendium: Analytisch-bibliographisches Repertorium der Werke Johann Sebastian Bachs (BC).* **Leipzig and Frankfurt, 1985– .**

The authors of the BC claim that this multi-volume analytical and bibliographic reference work on J.S. Bach's music goes well beyond the scope of Schmieder's BWV but that it is not meant to replace the older work. For the researcher, though, the BC, when it is complete, will be the first place to turn for information on all of Bach's music, as it already is for his vocal compositions.

The BC differs from the BWV in two principal ways. First, it is primarily concerned with the sources of and documentable facts about Bach's music. The entry for each composition directly cites the primary sources and documents for each assignment of authorship, dating, revision, and the like; the largest part of each entry is a compact but detailed description of the sources for each work. In this regard, the BC reflects the emphasis on source studies of Bach's music characteristic of the years between 1950 and 1985.

The second way in which the BC differs from the BWV lies in its comprehensive view of Bach's output, both surviving and lost. Like the BWV, it is organized by genre, but more specifically by the function of compositions—church cantatas, secular cantatas for each of several different kinds of events, and so on. Within work groups or subgroups, compositions are generally listed chronologically. Unlike the BWV, there is an entry in the BC for each identifiable individual work by Bach, including multiple versions of the "same" composition, as well as for lost and reconstructed works. For this reason, the BC will contain many more entries than the BWV.

As with the BWV, the main point of entry is the individual composition. (Note that each volume contains a concordance of BC and BWV numbers.) The fourth of the volumes covering Bach's vocal works also includes indexes of text incipits, of work titles and genre designations, of named characters, of instrumental movements, and of melodies quoted instrumentally. The final volume of the *Compendium* will also include detailed indexes of copyists, owners of sources, etc., giving access to the information in the BC from many other points of view.

The introductory material to the BC and to each section is presented both in German and in English, so English-speaking users should be able to find their way through the basic information in the entries, though some of the longer work histories require some command of German.

Each entry, besides giving information on scoring, texts, the work's history, sources, editions, and musical incipits, also cites important literature on each work. *Note that little literature before 1950 is cited; for earlier writings, one must consult the BWV.* Each section of the BC is also preceded by a bibliography of the most important general literature on the genre under consideration. Each volume after the first contains a list of addenda and corrigenda.

1.2 Bibliographies

The secondary literature on J.S. Bach and his music is vast, but fortunately the field is well served by bibliographies. Throughout this book, we suggest starting points for research on particular compositions and topics, but for more extensive coverage, one should consult the bibliographic tools listed in this section.

Christoph Wolff, ed. *Bach-Bibliographie: Nachdruck der Verzeichnisse des Schrifttums über Johann Sebastian Bach (Bach-Jahrbuch 1905–1984); mit einem Supplement und Register.* Cassel, 1985.

This volume reproduces the bibliographies from the *Bach-Jahrbuch* cited below through the one published in 1984. In addition, there is a chapter "Das Bachschrifttum 1910 bis 1944—eine Auswahlbibliographie" providing selective coverage of the gap in those compilations. The volume also contains a cumulative author index of all the bibliographies.

Max Schneider. "Verzeichnis der bisher erschienenen Literatur über Johann Sebastian Bach." *BJ* [2] (1905): 76–110.

Max Schneider. "Neues Material zum Verzeichnis der bisher erschienenen Literatur über Johann Sebastian Bach." *BJ* 7 (1910): 133–59.

Wolfgang Schmieder. "Das Bachschrifttum 1945–1952." *BJ* 40 (1953): 119–68.

Wolfgang Schmieder. "Das Bachschrifttum 1953–1957." *BJ* 45 (1958): 127–50.

Erhard Franke. "Das Bachschrifttum 1958–1962." *BJ* 53 (1967): 121–69.

Rosemarie Nestle. "Das Bachschrifttum 1963–1967." *BJ* 59 (1973): 91–150.

Rosemarie Nestle. "Das Bachschrifttum 1968–1972." *BJ* 62 (1976): 95–168.

Rosemarie Nestle. "Das Bachschrifttum 1973 bis 1977." *BJ* 66 (1980): 87–152.

Rosemarie Nestle. "Das Bachschrifttum 1978 bis 1980." *BJ* 70 (1984): 131–73.

Rosemarie Nestle. "Das Bachschrifttum 1981 bis 1985." *BJ* 75 (1989): 107–89.

Rosemarie Nestle. "Das Bachschrifttum 1986 bis 1990." *BJ* 80 (1994): 75–162.

The most comprehensive bibliographies of writings on Bach are these, published at intervals in the *Bach-Jahrbuch*. They are organized systematically by topic. Between the second of Max Schneider's compilations (covering to approximately 1909) and the first of the post-World-War bibliographies (starting in 1945) there is a gap, partly filled by a chapter in Wolff, *Bach-Bibliographie*.

These bibliographies also provide good coverage of reviews of important publications on Bach. The reviews are listed together with the reviewed item; be sure to look not only in the bibliography that includes the item you are interested in, but also in the corresponding place in the subsequent compilation to catch reviews that appeared later.

An on-line bibliography of writings on Bach has been established by Yo Tomita. It can be found at
http://www.music.qub.ac.uk/~tomita/bachbib.html

1.3 Dictionaries

Basic information on many topics—pieces, places, people, etc.—can be found in the following dictionaries. The first is particularly up to date and comprehensive.

Malcolm Boyd, ed. *Oxford composer companion: J.S. Bach*. Oxford, forthcoming.

Walter Kolneder. *Lübbes Bach Lexikon*. Bergisch Gladbach, 1982.

1.4 Other resources with strong bibliographies

Wolfgang Schmieder. *Thematisch-systematisches Verzeichnis der musik-alischen Werke von Johann Sebastian Bach: Bach-Werke-Verzeichnis (BWV).* **Wiesbaden, 1950, and reprints. 2d ed. 1990.**

Hans-Joachim Schulze and Christoph Wolff. *Bach Compendium: Ana-lytisch-bibliographisches Repertorium der Werke Johann Sebastian Bachs (BC).* **Leipzig and Frankfurt, 1985– .**

The BWV and the BC are among the most valuable sources of references to secondary literature (see *1.1 Basic reference tools*). Both works cite litera-ture relevant to each composition they list; in addition, the BC contains bibliographies of general literature on each genre (work group). Remember that the first edition of BWV covers literature to c.1950, BC after c.1950, and the second edition of BWV some of each.

Christoph Wolff and Walter Emery. "**Bach, Johann Sebastian.**" In *The New Grove dictionary of music and musicians,* **edited by Stanley Sadie. 20 vols. London, 1980.**

Christoph Wolff et al. *The New Grove Bach family.* **New York, 1983.**

Christoph Wolff et al. *Die Bach-Familie.* **Stuttgart, 1993.**

One of the strongest Bach bibliographies is found in the article on J.S. Bach in *The New Grove dictionary of music and musicians.* There are at least three versions of this article. The dictionary entry itself includes a bibliogra-phy organized by subject, in chronological order within each section. A slightly revised version, containing more recent literature, appears in the individual *New Grove* Bach volume. Finally, the revised German version of this volume contains an updated and substantially enlarged bibliography.

In many of the sections below we cite bibliographies of special topics in Bach research.

1.5 Surveys of Bach studies

From time to time, scholars involved in Bach studies have stepped back to consider the state of research and directions for the field. Here are a few of their writings, which are also useful surveys for new researchers.

A broad survey of Bach research, past and present, is offered in

Werner Neumann. *Aufgaben und Probleme der heutigen Bachforschung.* Berlin, 1979.

The most explosive years of Bach research are covered by
Walter Blankenburg. "Zwölf Jahre Bachforschung." *Acta musicologica* 37 (1965): 95–158.

Walter Blankenburg. "Die Bachforschung seit etwa 1965: Ergebnisse—Probleme—Aufgaben." *Acta musicologica* 50 (1978): 93–154; 54 (1982): 162–207; 55 (1983): 1–58.

The history of Bach scholarship in much of this period is surveyed in the context of the musicological enterprise in an insightful—if characteristically critical—way in
Joseph Kerman. *Contemplating music,* 50–55. Cambridge, Mass., 1985.

Hans-Joachim Schulze called for a systematic consideration of the eighteenth-century transmission of Bach's music in
Hans-Joachim Schulze. "Die Bach-Überlieferung: Plädoyer für ein notwendiges Buch." *Beiträge zur Musikwissenschaft* 17 (1975): 45–57.

Schulze went a long way toward answering this plea himself with
Hans-Joachim Schulze. *Studien zur Bach-Überlieferung im 18. Jahrhundert.* Leipzig, 1984.

Writings on the production of the Neue Bach-Ausgabe, its scope, and its editorial policies often reflect on Bach studies in general; see *6.2.3 Neue Bach-Ausgabe.*

1.6 Bach organizations

Here are the principal scholarly organizations devoted to Bach, their addresses, and their regular publications.

The American Bach Society, c/o secretary, Stephen A. Crist, Department of Music, Emory University, Atlanta, Georgia 30322. Publications: *Newsletter*, Bach perspectives.

Bach-Archiv, Postfach 101349, 04023 Leipzig, Germany. Publications: Neue Bach-Ausgabe (with Johann-Sebastian-Bach-Institut, Göttingen), *Leipziger Beiträge zur Bachforschung.*

Johann-Sebastian-Bach-Institut, Dahlmannstr. 14, 37073 Göttingen, Germany. Publication: Neue Bach-Ausgabe (with Bach-Archiv, Leipzig)

Neue Bachgesellschaft, Postfach 727, 04023 Leipzig, Germany. Publications: *Bach-Jahrbuch*, *Mitteilungsblatt*.

Riemenschneider Bach Institute, Baldwin-Wallace College, 275 Eastland Road, Berea, Ohio 44017–2088. Publication: *Bach: Journal of the Riemenschneider Bach Institute*.

2

Sources of secondary literature

Here we present journals, serials, essay collections, and other principal sources for writings on Bach. Obviously, literature on Bach appears in musical publications of all kinds. These listings are limited to publications devoted to Bach.

2.1 Periodicals

There are two periodicals devoted to Bach studies.

Bach-Jahrbuch, published annually in Leipzig by the Neue Bachgesell-schaft. Address: Postfach 727, 04007 Leipzig, Germany.

Note that there was a gap after the publication of Vol. 36 (1939), which was followed by Vol. 37, published in 1948 and dated 1940–48. There were also several combined volumes (1949–50, 1951–52, and 1963–64). The volumes are numbered as follows:

Vol. 1 (1904)–Vol. 36 (1939); Vol. 37 (1940–48); Vol. 38 (1949–50); Vol. 39 (1951–52); Vol. 40 (1953)–Vol. 49 (1962); Vol. 50 (1963–64); Vol. 51 (1965)– .

The contents of the first fifty volumes are listed and indexed in
    "Inhaltsverzeichnis der Jahrgänge 1–50 des Bach-Jahrbuches (1904 bis 1963–1964)." *BJ* 50 (1963–64): 70–108.

Selected essays from older issues are reprinted in
    Hans-Joachim Schulze, ed. *Aufsätze über Johann Sebastian Bach: Auswahl aus den Jahrgängen 1904–1939 des Bach-Jahrbuchs.* 2 vols. Cassel, 1985.

The *Bach-Jahrbuch* periodically publishes bibliographies of writings on Bach. See *1.2 Bibliographies.*

Bach: Journal of the Riemenschneider Bach Institute, usually published quarterly by the Riemenschneider Bach Institute, Baldwin-Wallace College, Berea, Ohio, since 1970. Address: Riemenschneider Bach Institute, Baldwin-Wallace College, 275 Eastland Road, Berea, Ohio 44017–2088.

The first twenty-two years' contents are indexed in
Bach Journal. Cumulative Index 1970–1992. [Berea, 1993].

2.2 Serials

There are many scholarly serials devoted to Bach. Here we list them and their volumes to date. Many are collections of essays by various authors, often representing papers presented at Bach conferences. (Collections are indicated here by the annotation [Essays].) The individual essays in these volumes are analyzed in the Bach bibliographies cited above. When looking for these volumes, note that some libraries catalogue them under the series title, some under the individual titles and authors/editors.

Bach perspectives, published by the University of Nebraska Press for the American Bach Society.

1. Russell Stinson, ed. Lincoln, 1995. [Essays]
2. George B. Stauffer, ed. *J.S. Bach, the Breitkopfs, and eighteenth-century music trade.* Lincoln, 1996. [Essays]
3. Michael Marissen, ed. *Creative responses to Bach from Mozart to Hindemith.* Lincoln, 1998. [Papers read at a conference, Berkeley, 1996]

Bach-Studien

1. Wilhelm Werker. *Studien über die Symmetrie im Bau der Fugen und die motivische Zusammengehörigkeit der Präludien und Fugen des "Wohltemperierten Klaviers" von Johann Sebastian Bach.* Leipzig, 1922.
2. Wilhelm Werker. *Die Matthäus-Passion.* Leipzig, 1923.
3. Werner Neumann. *J.S. Bachs Chorfuge: ein Beitrag zur Kompositionstechnik Bachs.* 3d ed. Leipzig, 1953.
4. Alfred Dürr. *Studien über die frühen Kantaten J.S. Bachs.* Leipzig, 1951.
5. Rudolf Eller and Hans-Joachim Schulze, eds. *Eine Sammlung von Aufsätzen.* Leipzig, 1975. [Essays. "Werner Neumann zum 65. Geburtstag"]

6. Peter Ahnsehl, Karl Heller and Hans-Joachim Schulze, eds. *Beiträge zum Konzertschaffen Johann Sebastian Bachs.* Leipzig, 1981. [Proceedings of a colloquium, Rostock, May 1979]
7. Reinhard Szeskus, ed. *Johann Sebastian Bach und die Aufklärung.* Leipzig, 1982. [Papers read at a conference, Leipzig, 1979]
8. Edwin R. Jacobi, ed. *Albert Schweitzers nachgelassene Manuskripte über die Verzierungen bei Johann Sebastian Bach: mit einer Einführung in die geplante Revision seines Buches über Johann Sebastian Bach.* Leipzig, 1984.
9. Reinhard Szeskus and Jürgen Asmus, eds. *Johann Sebastian Bachs Traditionsraum.* Leipzig, 1986. [Papers read at a colloquium, Leipzig, 1983. "Werner Neumann zum 80. Geburtstag gewidmet"]
10. Reinhard Szeskus, ed. *Johann Sebastian Bachs historischer Ort.* Wiesbaden, 1991. [Papers read at a conference, Leipzig, 1980s]

Bach studies

[1.] Don O. Franklin, ed. *Bach studies.* Cambridge, 1989. [Papers read at a conference, Flint, Mich., 1985]
2. Daniel R. Melamed, ed. *Bach studies 2.* Cambridge, 1995. [Essays]

Beiträge zur Bachforschung, published by the Nationale Forschungs- und Gedenkstätten Johann Sebastian Bach der DDR.

1. Karen Lehmann, ed. Leipzig, 1982. [Primarily papers read at a conference, Leipzig, 1981]
2. Karen Lehmann, ed. Leipzig, 1983. [Papers read at a conference, Leipzig, 1981]
3. Herbert Stiehl. *Das Innere der Thomaskirche zur Amtszeit Johann Sebastian Bachs.* Leipzig, 1984.
4. Karen Lehmann, ed. Leipzig, 1985. [Essays]
5. Werner Neumann and Christine Fröde. *Die Bach-Handschriften der Thomasschule Leipzig: Katalog.* Leipzig, 1986.
6. Karen Lehmann, ed. Leipzig, 1987. [Essays]
7. Armin Schneiderheinze, ed. *Johann Friedrich Doles: Anfangsgründe zum Singen.* Leipzig, 1989.
8. Andreas Glöckner. *Die Musikpflege an der Leipziger Neukirche zur Zeit Johann Sebastian Bachs.* Leipzig, 1990.
9/10. Karen Lehmann, ed. Leipzig, 1991. [Papers read at a conference, Leipzig, 1989]

Beiträge zur theologischen Bachforschung

1. Robin A. Leaver. *Bachs theologische Bibliothek: eine kritische Biblio-graphie mit einem Beitrag von Christoph Trautmann / Bach's theological library: a critical bibliography with an essay by Christoph Traut-mann*. Neuhausen-Stuttgart, 1983.
2. Elke Axmacher. *"Aus Liebe will mein Heyland sterben": Unter-suchungen zum Wandel des Passionsverständnisses im frühen 18. Jahr-hundert.* Neuhausen-Stuttgart, 1984.
3. Lothar Steiger and Renate Steiger. *Sehet, wir gehn hinauf gen Jerusalem: Johann Sebastian Bachs Kantaten auf den Sonntag Esto-mihi.* Göttingen, 1992.
4. Walter Blankenburg and Renate Steiger, eds. *Theologische Bach-Studien I.* Neuhausen-Stuttgart, 1987. [Essays]

Bulletin. Internationale Arbeitsgemeinschaft für theologische Bach-forschung

1. Renate Steiger, ed. *Sinnbildlichkeit in Text und Musik bei Johann Sebastian Bach.* Heidelberg, 1988. [Papers read at a conference, Heidelberg, 1987]
2. Renate Steiger, ed. *Parodie und Vorlage: zum Bachschen Parodie-verfahren und seiner Bedeutung für die Hermeneutik; die Messe BWV 234 und die Kantaten BWV 67, 179, 79 und 136.* Heidelberg, 1988. [Papers read at the Internationale Bachakademie Stuttgart, 1988]
3. Renate Steiger, ed. *Johann Sebastian Bachs Choralkantaten als Choral-Bearbeitungen.* Heidelberg, 1991. [Papers read at a confer-ence, Leipzig, 1990]
4. Renate Steiger, ed. *Die Seelsorgliche Bedeutung Johann Sebastian Bachs: Kantaten zum Thema Tod und Sterben.* Heidelberg, 1993. [Papers read at a conference, Schloß Beuggen, 1992]
5. Renate Steiger, ed. *"Wie freudig ist mein Herz, da Gott versöhnet ist"—Die Lehre von der Versöhnung in Kantaten und Orgelchorälen von Johann Sebastian Bach.* Heidelberg, 1995. [Papers read at a con-ference, Schlösschen Schönburg Hofgeismar, 1994]

Cöthener Bach-Hefte

1. 1981. [Essays]
2. 1983. [Exhibition catalogue; bibliography of Bach and Köthen]
3. 1985. [Essays]

4. 1986. *Beiträge des Kolloquiums der Bach-Gedenkstätte im Historischen Museum am 18. März 1985: "Hofkapellmeisteramt—Spätbarock—Frühaufklärung."* [Essays]
5. 1992. *Die Schloßkapelle zu Köthen und ihre Musikinstrumente.* [Essays]
6. 1994. *Festschrift zum Leopoldsfest (15. Köthener Bachfesttage): 23. bis 27. November 1994; zum 300. Geburtstag des Fürsten Leopold von Anhalt-Köthen (1694–1728).* [Essays]

Leipziger Beiträge zur Bachforschung

1. Hans-Joachim Schulze, Ulrich Leisinger and Peter Wollny. *Passionsmusiken im Umfeld Johann Sebastian Bachs / Bach unter den Diktaturen 1933–1945 und 1945–1989.* Hildesheim, 1995. [Papers read at a conference, Leipzig, 1994]
2. Ulrich Leisinger and Peter Wollny. *Die Bach-Quellen der Bibliotheken in Brüssel: Katalog mit einer Darstellung von Überlieferungsgeschichte und Bedeutung der Sammlungen Westphal, Fétis und Wagener.* Hildesheim, 1997.

Tübinger Bach-Studien

1. Georg von Dadelsen. *Bemerkungen zur Handschrift Johann Sebastian Bachs, seiner Familie und seines Kreises.* Trossingen, 1957.
2/3. Paul Kast. *Die Bach-Handschriften der Berliner Staatsbibliothek.* Trossingen, 1958.
4/5. Georg von Dadelsen. *Beiträge zur Chronologie der Werke Johann Sebastian Bachs.* Trossingen, 1958.
6. Doris Finke-Hecklinger. *Tanzcharaktere in Johann Sebastian Bachs Vokalmusik.* Trossingen, 1970.

2.3 Conference reports

Papers presented at scholarly conferences are often published in collections. Here we list Bach conferences with published proceedings, giving the place, date, and sponsoring organization where appropriate.

Lüneburg, 1950: Gesellschaft für Musikforschung

Hans Albrecht, Helmuth Osthoff and Walter Wiora, eds. Kongreß-Bericht: Gesellschaft für Musikforschung, Lüneburg, 1950. Cassel, 1950.

Leipzig, 1950: Gesellschaft für Musikforschung / 27. Bachfest der Neuen Bachgesellschaft

Walther Vetter, Ernst Hermann Meyer and Hans Heinrich Eggebrecht, eds. *Bericht über die wissenschaftliche Bachtagung der Gesellschaft für Musikforschung, Leipzig, 23. bis 26. Juli 1950.* Leipzig, 1951.

Leipzig, 1975: III. Internationales Bach-Fest der DDR / 50. Bachfest der Neuen Bachgesellschaft

Werner Felix, Winfried Hoffmann and Armin Schneiderheinze, eds. *Bericht über die wissenschaftliche Konferenz zum III. Internationalen Bach-Fest der DDR.* Leipzig, 1977.

Leipzig, 1977: Forschungskollektiv "Johann Sebastian Bach" an der Karl-Marx-Universität Leipzig

Reinhard Szeskus and Hans Grüss, eds. *Aufführungspraktische Probleme der Werke Johann Sebastian Bachs.* Leipzig, 1987.

Marburg, 1978: 53. Bachfest der Neuen Bachgesellschaft

Reinhold Brinkmann, ed. *Bachforschung und Bachinterpretation heute: Wissenschaftler und Praktiker im Dialog.* Cassel, 1981.

Rostock, 1979: Fachbereich Musikwissenschaft, Wilhelm-Pieck-Universität Rostock

Peter Ahnsehl, Karl Heller and Hans-Joachim Schulze, eds. *Beiträge zum Konzertschaffen Johann Sebastian Bachs.* Bach-Studien 6. Leipzig, 1981.

Leipzig, 1979: Forschungskollektiv "Johann Sebastian Bach" an der Karl-Marx-Universität Leipzig

Reinhard Szeskus, ed. *Johann Sebastian Bach und die Aufklärung.* Bach-Studien 7. Leipzig, 1982.

Graz, 1983: 58. Bachfest der Neuen Bachgesellschaft

Johann Trummer and Rudolf Flotzinger, eds. *Johann Sebastian Bach und Johann Joseph Fux: Bericht über das Symposion anläßlich des 58. Bachfestes der Neuen Bachgesellschaft 24.–29. Mai 1983 in Graz.* Cassel, 1985.

Leipzig, 1983: Forschungskollektiv "Johann Sebastian Bach" an der Karl-Marx-Universität Leipzig

Reinhard Szeskus and Jürgen Asmus, eds. *Johann Sebastian Bachs Traditionsraum.* Bach-Studien 9. Leipzig, 1986.

Cassel, 1984: 59. Bachfest der Neuen Bachgesellschaft

Kurt von Fischer, ed. *Bach im 20. Jahrhundert.* Cassel, 1985.

Stuttgart, 1985: Gesellschaft für Musikforschung / 60. Bachfest der Neuen Bachgesellschaft

Dietrich Berke and Dorothee Hanemann, eds. *Alte Musik als ästhetische Gegenwart—Bach, Händel, Schütz: Bericht über den internationalen musikwissenschaftlichen Kongreß Stuttgart 1985.* 2 vols. Cassel, 1987.

Flint, Michigan, 1985: University of Michigan-Flint

Don O. Franklin, ed. *Bach studies.* Cambridge, 1989.

Leipzig, 1985: V. Internationales Bachfest der DDR / 60. Bachfest der Neuen Bachgesellschaft

Winfried Hoffmann and Armin Schneiderheinze, eds. *Bach-Händel-Schütz-Ehrung der DDR 1985: Bericht über die wissenschaftliche Konferenz zum V. Internationalen Bachfest in Verbindung mit dem 60. Bachfest der Neuen Bachgesellschaft, Leipzig, 19. bis 27. März 1985.* Leipzig, 1988.

Hofstra University, 1985

Seymour L. Benstock, ed. *Johann Sebastian: a tercentenary celebration.* Westport, 1992.

Venice, 1985: Centro Tedesco di Studi Veneziani

Wolfgang Osthoff and Reinhard Wiesend, eds. *Bach und die italienische Musik / Bach e la musica italiana.* Venice, 1987.

Philadelphia, 1985: Basically Bach Festival

The Universal Bach: lectures celebrating the tercentenary of Bach's birthday, fall 1985. Philadelphia, 1986.

Vienna, 1985: Österreichische Gesellschaft für Musikwissenschaft

Ingrid Fuchs and Susanne Antonicek, eds. *Johann Sebastian Bach: Beiträge zur Wirkungsgeschichte.* Vienna, 1992.

Köthen, 1985: Historisches Museum

Beiträge des Kolloquiums der Bach-Gedenkstätte im Historischen Museum am 18. März 1985: "Hofkapellmeisteramt—Spätbarock—Frühaufklärung." Cöthener Bach-Hefte 4. Köthen, 1986.

Duisburg, 1986: 61. Bachfest der Neuen Bachgesellschaft

Christoph Wolff, ed. *Johann Sebastian Bachs Spätwerk und dessen Umfeld: Perspektiven und Probleme.* Cassel, 1988.

Reggio Emilia, 1986: Comune di Castelnovo ne' Monti, Amministrazione provinciale di Reggio Emilia, Istituto musicale "Claudio Merulo"

Daniela Iotti, ed. *Bach tra '700 e '900: aspetti tecnici e teorici.* Milan, 1988.

Leipzig, 1989: VI. Internationales Bachfest der DDR / 64. Bachfest der Neuen Bachgesellschaft

Karen Lehmann, ed. *Johann Sebastian Bach—Schaffenskonzeption—Werkidee—Textbezug.* Beiträge zur Bachforschung 9/10. Leipzig, 1991.

Leipzig, no date specified: Forschungskollektiv "Johann Sebastian Bach" an der Universität Leipzig

Reinhard Szeskus, ed. *Johann Sebastian Bachs historischer Ort.* Bach-Studien 10. Wiesbaden, 1991.

Munich, 1990: 65. Bachfest der Neuen Bachgesellschaft

Hans-Joachim Schulze and Christoph Wolff, eds. *Johann Sebastian Bach und der süddeutsche Raum: Aspekte der Wirkungsgeschichte Bachs.* Regensburg, 1991.

Rostock, 1990: Institut für Musikwissenschaft der Universität Rostock

Karl Heller and Hans-Joachim Schulze, eds. *Das Frühwerk Johann Sebastian Bachs: Kolloquium veranstaltet vom Institut für Musikwissenschaft der Universität Rostock 11.–13. September 1990.* Cologne, 1995.

Leipzig, 1994: 69. Bachfest der Neuen Bachgesellschaft

Hans-Joachim Schulze, Ulrich Leisinger and Peter Wollny, eds. *Passionsmusiken im Umfeld Johann Sebastian Bachs—Bach unter den Diktaturen 1933–1945 und 1945–1989.* Leipziger Beiträge zur Bachforschung 1. Hildesheim, 1995.

Dortmund, 1996: Universität Dortmund—Institut für Musik und ihre Didaktik

Martin Geck and Werner Breig, eds. *Bachs Orchesterwerke: Bericht über das 1. Dortmunder Bach-Symposion im Januar 1996.* Dortmund, forthcoming.

Berkeley, 1996: American Bach Society

Michael Marissen, ed. *Creative responses to Bach from Mozart to Hindemith.* Bach perspectives 3. Lincoln, 1998.

2.4 Festival publications

Each year, the Neue Bachgesellschaft holds a festival consisting largely of concerts and recitals. In conjunction with these events, a program book (Bachfestbuch) is published, often containing program notes and essays well above the usual level of such writings. The contents of these books are indexed in the *Bach-Jahrbuch* bibliographies (see *1.2 Bibliographies*). In conjunction with these Bach festivals, the Neue Bachgesellschaft sometimes (but not always) sponsors a scholarly conference, the published proceedings of which are listed in *2.3 Conference reports*.

For addresses given at the Berlin Bachtage, see *2.6 Other essay collections*.

2.5 Festschrifts

Several volumes in honor of senior scholars consist entirely or largely of essays on Bach.

Walter Blankenburg

Martin Geck, ed. *Bach-Interpretationen.* Göttingen, 1969. ["Diese Aufsätze sind Walter Blankenburg zum 65. Gerburtstag gewidmet."]

Paul Brainard

John Knowles, ed. *Critica musica: essays in honor of Paul Brainard.* Amsterdam, 1996.

Georg von Dadelsen

Thomas Kohlhase and Volker Scherliess, eds. *Festschrift Georg von Dadelsen zum 60. Geburtstag.* Neuhausen-Stuttgart, 1978.

Kollegium des Johann-Sebastian-Bach-Instituts Göttingen, ed. *Acht kleine Präludien und Studien über Bach: Georg von Dadelsen zum 70. Geburtstag am 17. November 1988.* Wiesbaden, 1992.

Alfred Dürr

BJ 64 (1978). ["Alfred Dürr zum 60. Geburtstag am 3. März 1978 gewidmet"]

Wolfgang Rehm, ed. *Bachiana et alia musicologica: Festschrift Alfred Dürr zum 65. Geburtstag am 3. März 1983.* Cassel, 1983.

Gerhard Herz

Robert L. Weaver et al., eds. *Essays on the music of J.S. Bach and other divers subjects: a tribute to Gerhard Herz.* Louisville, 1981.

Arthur Mendel

Robert L. Marshall, ed. *Studies in Renaissance and Baroque music in honor of Arthur Mendel.* Hackensack, 1974.

Werner Neumann

Rudolf Eller and Hans-Joachim Schulze, eds. *Eine Sammlung von Aufsätzen: Werner Neumann zum 65. Geburtstag.* Bach-Studien 5. Leipzig, 1975.

Reinhard Szeskus and Jürgen Asmus, eds. *Johann Sebastian Bachs Traditionsraum.* Leipzig, 1986. [Papers read at a colloquium, Leipzig, 1983. "Werner Neumann zum 80. Geburtstag gewidmet"]

William H. Scheide

Paul Brainard and Ray Robinson, eds. *A Bach tribute: essays in honor of William H. Scheide.* Cassel, 1993.

Ulrich Siegele

Rudolf Faber et al., eds. *Festschrift Ulrich Siegele zum 60. Geburtstag.* Cassel, 1991.

Friedrich Smend

Festschrift für Friedrich Smend zum 70. Geburtstag. Berlin, 1963.

2.6 Other essay collections

Karl Matthaei, ed. *Internationale Bach-Gesellschaft Schaffhausen: Bach Gedenkschrift, 1950.* Zurich, 1950. [Essays]

Walter Blankenburg, ed. *Johann Sebastian Bach.* Wege der Forschung 170. Darmstadt, 1970. [Essays reprinted from other sources]

Martin Petzoldt, ed. *Bach als Ausleger der Bibel: theologische und musikwissenschaftliche Studien zum Werk Johann Sebastian Bachs.* Göttingen, 1985. [Essays]

Peter Williams, ed. *Bach, Handel, Scarlatti: tercentenary essays.* Cambridge, 1985. [Essays]

Bachtage Berlin: Vorträge 1970 bis 1981—Sammelband. Edited by Günther Wagner. Neuhausen-Stuttgart, 1985.

A little more than a decade's worth of addresses (not all on Bach) given in connection with the annual Berlin Bachtage.

George Stauffer and Ernest May, eds. *J.S. Bach as organist: his instruments, music, and performance practices.* Bloomington, 1986. [Essays]

2.7 Individuals' collected writings

The writings of several of the most prolific authors on Bach have been reissued in collections.

Walter Blankenburg. *Kirche und Musik: gesammelte Aufsätze zur Geschichte der gottesdienstlichen Musik,* edited by Erich Hübner and Renate Steiger. Göttingen, 1979.

Friedrich Blume. *Syntagma musicologicum,* edited by Anna Amalie Abert and Martin Ruhnke. Cassel, 1963.

Friedrich Blume. *Syntagma musicologicum II: gesammelte Reden und Schriften 1962–72,* edited by Anna Amalie Abert and Martin Ruhnke. Cassel, 1973.

Georg von Dadelsen. *Über Bach und anderes: Aufsätze und Vorträge 1957–1982,* edited by Arnold Feil and Thomas Kohlhase. Laaber, 1983.

Alfred Dürr. *Im Mittelpunkt Bach: ausgewählte Aufsätze und Vorträge,* edited by Kollegium des Johann-Sebastian-Bach-Instituts Göttingen. Cassel, 1988.

Wilhelm Ehmann. *Voce et Tuba: gesammelte Reden und Aufsätze 1934–1974,* edited by Dietrich Berke, Christiane Bernsdorff-Englebrecht and Helmut Kornemann. Cassel, 1976.

Gerhard Herz. *Essays on J.S. Bach.* Ann Arbor, 1985.

Includes a translation of the author's dissertation, "Johann Sebastian Bach im Zeitalter des Rationalismus und der Frühromantik." Zurich, 1934.

Robert L. Marshall. *The music of Johann Sebastian Bach: the sources, the style, the significance. New York,* 1989.

Friedrich Smend. *Bach-Studien: gesammelte Reden und Aufsätze,* edited by Christoph Wolff. Cassel, 1969.

Christoph Wolff. *Bach: essays on his life and music.* Cambridge, Mass., 1991.

2.8 Journal issues

Many journal issues were devoted to Bach in 1985. For a list see
Russell Stinson. "Bach tercentenary issues of periodicals: a selected bibliography." *Bach* 17, no. 4 (1986): 17–23.

3

Bach's life

3.1 The Bach family

3.1.1 Ancestors

General

In 1735, his fiftieth year, J.S. Bach made a genealogy of the Bach family.

> **"Ursprung der musicalisch-Bachischen Familie." Transcribed in *Dok* I/184, with additional notes in *Dok* III, p. 647; *BR*, 203–11.**

This genealogy assigns numbers to various (male) members of the family, and this numbering system, augmented in *New Grove*, is still used to distinguish family members. On the family in general and on individual members, see

> **New Grove, "Bach family" and individual entries for family members.**

The following two general works on the Bach family are outdated but still useful:

> **Karl Geiringer and Irene Geiringer. *The Bach family: seven generations of creative genius*. New York, 1954.**

> **Percy M. Young. *The Bachs, 1500–1850*. London, 1970.**

Special studies of older Bachs

Two older members of the family have been studied particularly for their musical connections to J.S. Bach.

Johann Christoph Bach (1671–1721) was J.S. Bach's older brother, with whom he lived and studied as a child. The basic study is

> **Hans-Joachim Schulze. "Johann Christoph Bach (1671 bis 1721), 'Organist und Schul Collega in Ohrdruf,' Johann Sebastian Bachs erster Lehrer." *BJ* 71 (1985): 55–81.**

He was also the copyist of two important sources of J.S. Bach's early keyboard compositions; see

Robert Stephen Hill. "The Möller Manuscript and the Andreas Bach Book: two keyboard anthologies from the circle of the young Johann Sebastian Bach." Ph.D. diss. Harvard University, 1987.

Robert Hill, ed. *Keyboard music from the Andreas Bach Book and the Möller Manuscript.* Cambridge, Mass., 1991.

Johann Ludwig Bach (1677–1731) was a cousin of J.S. Bach, who copied and performed eighteen of Johann Ludwig's church cantatas. On J.S. Bach's contact with this repertory, see

William H. Scheide. "Johann Sebastian Bachs Sammlung von Kantaten seines Vetters Johann Ludwig Bach." *BJ* 46 (1959): 52–94; 48 (1961): 5–24; 49 (1962): 5–32.

The Altbachisches Archiv

J.S. Bach owned—and possibly assembled—a collection of old family music known as the Altbachisches Archiv. On the collection and its history see

Daniel R. Melamed. "J.S. Bach and the German motet," 39–129. Ph.D. diss. Harvard University, 1989.

Much of the music from the collection, together with related repertory, is published in

Max Schneider, ed. *Altbachisches Archiv.* Das Erbe deutscher Musik 1/2. Leipzig, 1935.

3.1.2 Wives

Bach's first wife, Maria Barbara was a Bach by birth, the youngest daughter of Johann Michael Bach; see the literature on him (*3.1.1 Ancestors*) and on the town of Gehren in Thuringia (*3.5.1 Thuringia in general*).

His second wife was born Anna Magdalena Wilcke. On her role as copyist, see *5.1.3 Bach's copyists;* as inheritor of some of J.S. Bach's music, see *5.2.2 Bach's heirs.* On her family and youth, see

Christoph Schubart. "Anna Magdalena Bach: neue Beiträge zu ihrer Herkunft und ihren Jugendjahren." *BJ* 40 (1953): 29–50.

3.1.3 Children

Four of Bach's sons (Wilhelm Friedemann, Carl Philipp Emanuel, Johann Christoph Friedrich, and Johann Christian) were prolific and important composers on whom there is extensive literature. We present basic tools and literature particularly relevant to J.S. Bach studies. See also the biographical articles, worklists, and bibliographies in *New Grove*. On the inheritance by Bach's children of their father's music and their role in its transmission, see *5.2.1 Bach's estate and its division* and *5.2.2 Bach's heirs*. On their role as copyists and musical assistants to their father, see *5.1.3 Bach's copyists*.

Wilhelm Friedemann Bach (1710–1784)

The fullest biography (with a catalogue of works), outdated but still influential, is

Martin Falck. *Wilhelm Friedemann Bach*. 2d. ed. Leipzig, 1919.

For a recent survey of the works and their sources and a revision of Falck's catalogue, see

Peter Wollny. "Studies in the music of Wilhelm Friedemann Bach: sources and style." Ph.D. diss. Harvard University, 1993.

There is no complete edition of W.F. Bach's compositions.

On Wilhelm Friedemann's performances of his father's cantatas, see
Peter Wollny. "Wilhelm Friedemann Bach's Halle performances of cantatas by his father." In *Bach studies 2*, edited by Daniel R. Melamed, 202–28. Cambridge, 1995.

Carl Philipp Emanuel Bach (1714–1788)

A basic biography is

Hans-Günter Ottenberg. *Carl Philipp Emanuel Bach*. Leipzig, 1982. Translated by Philip J. Whitmore as *C.P.E. Bach*. Oxford, 1987.

The old thematic catalogue by Wotquenne has been succeeded by the less than thoroughly systematic

E. Eugene Helm. *Thematic catalogue of the works of Carl Philipp Emanuel Bach*. New Haven, 1989.

A complete edition of C.P.E. Bach's compositions is under way:

Rachel W. Wade, gen. ed. *Carl Philipp Emanuel Bach edition*. Oxford, 1989– .

The three catalogues of material from C.P.E. Bach's estate are extremely important sources in Bach research; see *5.2.2 Bach's heirs*. C.P.E. Bach's obituary of his father is printed as *Dok* III/666 and *BR*, 215–24, and several of his letters to Forkel, which were sources for the latter's biography of J.S. Bach, also appear in *Dok* III and *BR*.

On C.P.E. Bach's performances of his father's music, see
Joshua Rifkin. "'. . . Wobey aber die Singstimmen hinlänglich besetzt seyn müssen . . .': zum Credo der h-Moll-Messe in der Aufführung Carl Philipp Emanuel Bachs." *Basler Jahrbuch für historische Musikpraxis* 9 (1985): 157–72.

Johann Christoph Friedrich Bach (1732–95)

The standard biography and worklist are
Hannsdieter Wohlfarth. *Johann Christoph Friedrich Bach: ein Komponist im Vorfeld der Klassik.* **Bern, 1971.**

There is no complete edition of J.C.F. Bach's compositions.

Johann Christian Bach (1735–82)

The standard biography, with a worklist, is
Charles Sanford Terry. *John Christian Bach.* **London, 1929. 2d ed. with a Foreword by H.C.R. Landon. London, 1967.**

J.C. Bach's complete works are being published in
Ernest Warburton, gen. ed. *The collected works of Johann Christian Bach 1735–1782.* **New York, 1984– .**

This edition will include a thematic catalogue.

3.2 Documentation

3.2.1 Documents

The primary documents of Bach's life are transcribed and annotated in detail in
Werner Neumann and Hans-Joachim Schulze, eds. *Bach-Dokumente. Band I: Schriftstücke von der Hand Johann Sebastian Bachs.* **Cassel and Leipzig, 1963. [***Dok***I]**

Werner Neumann and Hans-Joachim Schulze, eds. *Bach-Dokumente.* *Band II: Fremdschriftliche und gedruckte Dokumente zur Lebensgeschichte Johann Sebastian Bachs 1685–1750.* Cassel and Leipzig, 1969. [*Dok* II]

Hans-Joachim Schulze, ed. *Bach-Dokumente. Band III: Dokumente zum Nachwirken Johann Sebastian Bachs 1750–1800.* Cassel and Leipzig, 1972. [*Dok* III]

The first volume covers writings in Bach's hand, the second and third (divided at Bach's death) printed documents and those written by others. They are organized chronologically, with the first volume also divided by type of document (letters, receipts, etc.). The third volume contains an extensive index and corrigenda, as well as documents belonging in volumes I and II but discovered after the publication of the earlier volumes. (A fourth volume contains pictorial documents; see *3.2.2 Iconography.*)

Many documents are available in English translations in

Hans T. David and Arthur Mendel, eds. *The Bach reader.* Rev. ed. New York, 1966.

The versions here should be used with the same caution as with any other translations. Also included is an early nineteenth-century English translation of Johann Nicolaus Forkel's influential Bach biography (see *3.3.1 Primary and early biographies*). A revision of the *The Bach reader* by Christoph Wolff is in progress.

Many of the most important documents have been reprinted in

Hans-Joachim Schulze, ed. *Johann Sebastian Bach: Leben und Werk in Dokumenten.* Leipzig, 1975.

A few Bach documents have generated their own interpretive literature. On the "Short but most necessary draft for a well-appointed church music," see the literature in *9.1 Vocal forces.* On the documents concerning Bach's students and his teaching, see *4.1 Bach's teaching and students.* On the famous polemic between Scheibe and Birnbaum, see *11.4 Reception.* On Bach's estate, see *5.2.1 Bach's estate and its division* and *4.2 Bach's library.* On C.P.E. Bach's obituary of his father, see *3.3.1 Primary and early biographies.*

Inevitably, documents have been discovered since the publication of the three volumes of documents. Here is a list of the most important belonging to volumes I and II, together with citations of literature describing and discussing them.

Volume I

1713/14: Record of Bach's expenses in connection with his application for the organist's post at the Marienkirche in Halle
Peter Wollny. "Bachs Bewerbung um die Organistenstelle an der Marienkirche zu Halle und ihr Kontext." *BJ* 80 (1994): 25–39.

28 July 1726: Letter to Georg Erdmann
Grigorij Ja. Pantijelew. "Johann Sebastian Bachs Briefe an Georg Erdmann: nebst Beiträgen zur Lebensgeschichte von Bachs Jugendfreund." *BJ* 71 (1985): 83–97.

5 April 1734: Testimonial for Paul Christian Stoll(e)
Reinhold Krause. "Noch ein unbekanntes Zeugnis Johann Sebastian Bachs." *BJ* 64 (1978): 73–77.

1746–49: Receipts for the "Nathanisches Legat"
Hans-Joachim Schulze. "Vier unbekannte Quittungen J.S. Bachs und ein Briefauszug Jacob von Stählins." *BJ* 59 (1973): 88–90.

Hans Moldenhauer. "J.S. Bach und das Nathanische Legat: bisher unveröffentlichte Quittungstexte." *Neue Zeitschrift für Musik* 141 (1980): 353.

18 December 1747: Receipt for the rental of a keyboard
Christoph Trautmann. "Unregistriertes Dokument belegt Graf Wrbna als österreichischen Bach-Schüler." *Bachfestbuch Graz*, 1983: 81–86.

12 January 1748: Testimonial for Heinrich Andreas Cuntzius, organ maker
Wolf Hobohm. "Ein unbekanntes Gutachen Johann Sebastian Bachs." *BJ* 63 (1977): 135–38.

Various: Baptismal records for Bach's children (two documents are in Bach's handwriting)
Herbert Stiehl. "Taufzettel für Bachs Kinder—ein Dokumentenfund." *BJ* 65 (1979): 7–18.

Volume II

12 April 1717: Room receipt for "ConcertMeister Bach" in Gotha
Eva-Maria Ranft. "Ein unbekannter Aufenthalt Johann Sebastian Bachs in Gotha?" *BJ* 71 (1985): 165–66.

7 February 1739: Reference to Bach and his music
George B. Stauffer. "Christian Gottlieb Zieglers 'Anleitung zur musikalischen Composition': ein Bach-Dokument aus der New York Public Library." *BJ* 74 (1988): 185–89.

20 May 1747: Newspaper report on Bach's Potsdam visit
Heinz Scior. "Bachs Potsdam-Besuch in den 'Franckfurter Gazetten.'" *BJ* **78 (1992): 81–83.**

3 October 1749: Letter from Johann Jacob Donati to the Leipzig *Oberpostsekretär* Georg Gottfried Günther on the use of Bach as organ examiner
Wolfram Hackel. "Johann Sebastian Bachs Ruf als Orgelsachverständiger: zu einem Brief Johann Jacob Donatis d.J. aus dem Jahre 1749." Beiträge zur Bachforschung 6 (1987): 92–95.

Various: Baptismal records for Bach's children
Herbert Stiehl. "Taufzettel für Bachs Kinder—ein Dokumentenfund." *BJ* **65 (1979): 7–18.**

3.2.2 Iconography

Many portraits have been put forward as representing Bach. The only authentic image of Bach is the portrait by Elias Gottlob Haussmann, known in a version from 1746 (now in Leipzig) and one from 1748 (Princeton, New Jersey).

A possibly authentic painting of Bach and his sons is discussed in an editor's note:
Nicholas Kenyon. "A Bach family portrait?" *Early Music* **13 (1985): 164.**

For literature on Bach iconography, including discussions of the provenence and authenticity of known portraits and information on lost portraits, see the picture books cited below and
Hans Raupach. *Das wahre Bildnis des Johann Sebastian Bach: Bericht und Dokumente*. Munich, 1983.

Images of Bach's world have been assembled in several collections. Particularly strong Bach picture collections—portraits, depictions of buildings and cities, reproductions of documents, etc.—are found in
Werner Neumann, ed. *Bilddokumente zur Lebensgeschichte Johann Sebastian Bachs / Pictorial documents of the life of Johann Sebastian Bach*. Bach-Dokumente 4. Leipzig and Cassel, 1979.

Barbara Schwendowius and Wolfgang Dömling, eds. *Johann Sebastian Bach: Zeit, Leben, Wirken*. Cassel, 1976. English translation as *Johann Sebastian Bach: life, times, influence*. Cassel, 1977.

Images connected with Bach's religious and liturgical life are collected in
> **Martin Petzoldt.** *Ehre sei dir Gott gesungen: Bilder und Texte zu Bachs Leben als Christ und seinem Wirken für die Kirche.* **2d ed. Göttingen, 1990.**

3.3 Biographies of J.S. Bach

An overwhelming number of Bach biographies, few of them adding much to the archival researches of earlier studies, has appeared in the twentieth century. One of the more readable and probably the best of these is
> **Malcolm Boyd.** *Bach.* **2d. ed. Oxford, 1995.**

Less reader-friendly but extremely useful is
> **Christoph Wolff and Walter Emery. "Bach, Johann Sebastian." In** *The New Grove dictionary of music and musicians,* **edited by Stanley Sadie. 20 vols. London, 1980. Rev. in Christoph Wolff et al.** *The New Grove Bach family.* **New York, 1983. Further rev. in translation as** *Die Bach-Familie.* **Stuttgart, 1993.**

For a particularly good short study, see
> **Martin Geck.** *Johann Sebastian Bach: mit Selbstzeugnissen und Bilddokumenten.* **Reinbek bei Hamburg, 1993.**

For a recent study of Bach's early career, see
> **Konrad Küster.** *Der junge Bach.* **Stuttgart, 1996.**

For a survey of older biographies, see
> **Albert Riemenschneider. "Bach biographies and their authors 1732–1935."** *Music Book* **7 (1953): 381–92.**

3.3.1 Primary and early biographies

In this and the next section we mention the most important biographies based on original research into Bach's life and personality.

Obituary

Bach's obituary notice (Nekrolog), written by his son Carl Philipp Emanuel and his students Johann Friedrich Agricola and Lorenz Mizler, is an interesting account of selected aspects of his life. All biographical research on Bach is heavily indebted to it. The notice was first printed in

Lorenz Christoph Mizler [von Kolof]. *Neu eröffnete musikalische Bibliothek,* IV/1, 158–76. Leipzig, 1754. [Transcribed in *BJ* 17 (1920): 11–29 and *Dok* III/666; *BR,* 215–24]

Forkel

Johann Nikolaus Forkel. *Ueber Johann Sebastian Bachs Leben, Kunst und Kunstwerke: für patriotische Verehrer echter musikalischer Kunst.* Leipzig, 1802, and reprints.

This is the first extended study on Bach, partly based on information garnered from correspondence with Bach's sons Carl Philipp Emanuel and Wilhelm Friedemann. It is more a critical appreciation of Bach's art and works than a "life" in the biographical sense. Some editions of the German version modernize Forkel's expressions, not always accurately; it is best to consult a facsimile of the original publication.

An anonymous translation appeared as

[J.N.] Forkel. *Life of John Sebastian Bach, with a critical view of his compositions.* London, 1820. Reprinted as "On Johann Sebastian Bach's life, genius, and works" in *BR,* 293–356.

For a better translation (with notes and appendices by the translator), see

Johann Nikolaus Forkel. *Johann Sebastian Bach: his life, art, and work,* translated and edited by Charles Sanford Terry. London, 1920, and reprints.

3.3.2 Later biographies

Spitta

Philipp Spitta. *Johann Sebastian Bach,* 2 vols. Leipzig, 1873–80, and reprints. Translated by Clara Bell and John Alexander Fuller-Maitland as *Johann Sebastian Bach: his work and influence on the music of Germany, 1685–1750.* 3 vols. London, 1884–85, and reprints.

A monumental study of Bach's life and works. It set formidable standards for thoroughness in documentary research, and all subsequent Bach scholarship has been in its shadow. Nothing approaching its scope has since been attempted.

Readers should be sure to notice Spitta's various appendices, supplementary materials, and lists of corrections, not all of which appear in the English version.

Because the English translation's accuracy often leaves a great deal to be desired, those doing advanced work should always check it against the original. The English version has its own scholarly value, though, as it contains some author's revisions that were not incorporated into subsequent printings of the German version.

Other biographies

Here we list the most important biographies after Forkel and Spitta that were based on original documentary research or that, though not offering much in the way of new archival material, have had an especially extensive readership and influence.

Forkel's information is essentially repeated in

C.L. Hilgenfeldt. *Johann Sebastian Bachs Leben, Wirken und Werke: ein Beitrag zur Kunstgeschichte des achtzehnten Jahrhunderts.* Leipzig, 1850.

A summary in English of Forkel and Hilgenfeldt with negligible additions appeared as

Edward Francis Rimbault, ed. *Johann Sebastian Bach: his life and writings; adapted from the German of Hilgenfeldt and Forkel, with additions from original sources.* London, 1869.

The first biography employing modern methods of archival research— soon after, however, eclipsed by Spitta's—is

C.H. Bitter. *Johann Sebastian Bach.* 2 vols. Berlin, 1865. Rev. and exp. ed., 1881. Translated by Janet E. Kay-Shuttleworth as *The life of J. Sebastian Bach: an abridged translation from the German of C.H. Bitter.* London, 1873.

Widely read critical assessments of Bach that draw only on Spitta for their biographical materials are

Albert Schweitzer. *J.S. Bach, le musicien-poète.* Leipzig, 1905. Exp. version in German as *J.S. Bach.* Leipzig, 1908, and reprints. Latter translated by Ernest Newman, with minor additions by the author, as *J.S. Bach.* Leipzig and New York, 1911, and reprints.

André Pirro. *J.S. Bach.* Paris, 1906 [in French]. Translated by Mervyn Savill as *J.S. Bach.* New York, 1957.

An elegantly written study of Bach's artistic personality, but not featuring any new documentary material, is

Charles Hubert Hastings Parry. *Johann Sebastian Bach: the story of the development of a great personality.* Rev. ed. London, 1934, and reprints.

The results of new archival research, undertaken by the author and gleaned from the literature on Bach, appeared in

Charles Sanford Terry. *Bach: a biography.* **2d ed. London, 1933, and reprints.**

3.3.3 *The Bach image*

The image of Bach as Great Pious Lutheran was first projected by

C.H. Bitter. *Johann Sebastian Bach.* **2 vols. Berlin, 1865. Rev. and exp. ed., 1881. Translated by Janet E. Kay-Shuttleworth as** *The life of J. Sebastian Bach: an abridged translation from the German of C.H. Bitter.* **London, 1873.**

and put forth forcefully by Philipp Spitta (see *3.3.2 Later biographies*). It was also the concentrated subject of the widely read monograph

Hans Preuß. *Johann Sebastian Bach, der Lutheraner.* **Erlangen. 1935.**

and of many studies by the theologian and Bach scholar Friedrich Smend.

Following upon the new chronological research of Alfred Dürr and Georg von Dadelsen in the 1950s (see *7.2.2 Chronologies of Bach's vocal music*), Friedrich Blume radically questioned this view, now seeing Bach as a begrudging, impious church musician and a sort of proto-Marxist. See

Friedrich Blume. "**Umrisse eines neuen Bach-Bildes: Vortrag für das Bachfest der internationalen Bach-Gesellschaft in Mainz, 1. Juni 1962; Vorabdruck.**" *Musica* **16 (1962): 169–76, and reprints. Translated as** "**Outlines of a new picture of Bach.**" *Music and Letters* **44 (1963): 214–27. Reprinted in** *Twentieth-century views of music history,* **edited by William Hays, 225–38. New York, 1972.**

An avalanche of scholarly protests immediately followed. The most important of these are

Alfred Dürr. "**Zum Wandel des Bach-Bildes: zu Friedrich Blumes Mainzer Vortrag.**" *Musik und Kirche* **32 (1962): 145–52. [cf.** "**Antwort von Friedrich Blume,**" **153–56]**

Friedrich Smend. "**Was bleibt? Zu Friedrich Blumes Bach-Bild.**" *Der Kirchenmusiker* **13 (1962): 178–88. Also as pamphlet. Berlin, 1962.**

For more detailed responses, taking into account, among other things, the discovery of Bach's personal Bible with extensive hand-penned annotations, and now providing a more nuanced version of the older image, see

Christoph Trautmann. "'Calovii Schrifften. 3. Bände' aus Johann Sebastian Bachs Nachlass und ihre Bedeutung für das Bild des lutherischen Kantors Bach." *Musik und Kirche* 39 (1969): 145–160. Translated as "J.S. Bach: new light on his faith." *Concordia Theological Monthly* 42 (1971): 88–99.

Gerhard Herz. "Toward a new image of Bach." *Bach* 1, no. 4 (1970): 9–27; and 2, no. 1 (1971): 7–28. Reprinted in his *Essays on J.S. Bach*, 149–84. Ann Arbor, 1985.

A related but somewhat different issue concerns Bach's socially progressive versus reactionary outlooks. For an exceedingly clever and influential essay arguing for the former, see

Theodor W. Adorno. "Bach gegen seine Liebhaber verteidigt." *Merkur* 5 (1951): 535–46. Translated by Samuel Weber and Shierry Weber as "Bach defended against his devotees." In Adorno, *Prisms*, 133–46. London, 1967, and reprints.

Adorno's view—that Bach's life and music appear to be trapped in what he called the Middle Ages while they in essence look ahead to the Enlightenment—was developed by

Susan McClary. "The blasphemy of talking politics during Bach year." In *Music and society: the politics of composition, performance and reception*, edited by Richard Leppert and Susan McClary, 13–62. Cambridge, 1987.

This view of Bach as Enlightenment-oriented has been questioned biographically and musically in

Michael Marissen. *The social and religious designs of J.S. Bach's Brandenburg Concertos*, 111–19. Princeton, 1995.

Michael Marissen. "The theological character of J.S. Bach's *Musical Offering*." In *Bach studies 2*, edited by Daniel R. Melamed, 85–106. Cambridge, 1995.

See also

Laurence Dreyfus. "Bach as critic of Enlightenment." In his *Bach and the patterns of invention*, 219–44. Cambridge, Mass., 1996.

The St. Thomas School rector Johann August Ernesti, who was to become a famous Enlightenment biblical scholar, had an extremely strained relationship with Bach; for a study taking this to involve a clash of pro- and anti-Enlightenment sentiments, see

Paul S. Minear. "J.S. Bach and J.A. Ernesti: a case study in exegetical and theological conflict." In *Our common history as Christians: essays in honor of Albert C. Outler,* edited by John Deschner et al., 131–55. New York, 1975.

Pointing back to the sort of Bach image projected by Spitta and followers, the following authors study Bach's newly discovered personal Bible with his handwritten annotations for their biographical implications:

Renate Steiger. "Bach und die Bibel: einige Anstreichungen Bachs in seiner Calov-Bibel als Selbstzeugnisse gelesen." *Musik und Kirche* 57 (1987): 119–26.

Howard H. Cox. "Bach's conception of his office." *Bach* 20, no. 1 (1989): 22–30.

The notion that Bach held "Pietist" (anti-Orthodox Lutheran) views is often put forward; there is, however, considerable misunderstanding of what Pietism is and what Bach's relationship to it was. The problems are carefully sorted out in

Robin A. Leaver. "Bach and Pietism: similarities today." *Concordia Theological Quarterly* 55 (1991): 5–22.

For further consideration of whether Bach as artist should be considered progressive or backward-looking, see

Robert L. Marshall. "Bach the progressive: observations on his later works." *Musical Quarterly* 62 (1976): 313–57. Rev. in his *The music of Johann Sebastian Bach: the sources, the style, the significance,* 23–58. New York, 1989.

Frederick Neumann. "Bach: progressive or conservative and the authorship of the Goldberg aria." *Musical Quarterly* 71 (1985): 281–94. Rev. in his *New essays on performance practice,* 195–208. Ann Arbor, 1989.

Marshall argues that to the extent Bach allowed himself in the 1730s and '40s to be influenced by the latest developments in musical fashion (particularly the so-called *galant* styles), he can be characterized as progressive. Neumann argues that Bach actually made limited and aesthetically unsuccessful forays into the *galant* and that a conservative view of Bach is more fitting.

For a moderate, Eastern-bloc socialist reading of Bach's biography, see Walther Siegmund-Schultze. *Johann Sebastian Bach.* Leipzig, 1976.

On the notion that Bach was a social climber, see

Ulrich Siegele. "'Ich habe fleissig sein müssen . . .': zur Vermittlung von Bachs sozialem und musikalischem Charakter." *Musik und Kirche* 61 **(1991): 73–78. Also in Beiträge zur Bachforschung 9/10 (1991): 13–19. Translated by Gerhard Herz as "'I had to be industrious . . .': thoughts about the relationship between Bach's social and musical character."** *Bach* 22, no. 2 (1991): 5–12.

For an image of Bach as inexplicable and unknowable, see

Wolfgang Hildesheimer. *Der ferne Bach: eine Rede.* **Frankfurt am Main, 1985.**

3.4 Chronology of Bach's life

The following pamphlet, based largely on the volumes of the *Bach-Dokumente* and on studies of the chronology of Bach's vocal music, presents a chronology of the documented events of Bach's life and his known performances.

Bach-Archiv Leipzig. *Kalendarium zur Lebensgeschichte Johann Sebastian Bachs.* **2d ed. Leipzig, 1979.**

For studies of the chronology of Bach's music and its sources, see *7.2.2 Chronologies of Bach's vocal music* and *8.1.1 General topics in Bach's instrumental music.*

3.5 Places and their biographical issues

In this section we present literature about the places in which Bach lived and worked or to which he made significant visits. We also include some references to general works on the musical history of these places. Note that there are brief but useful articles on most of these places, with bibliographies, in *New Grove.*

A useful guide to touring Bach cities and towns is

Martin Petzoldt. *Bachstätten aufsuchen.* **Leipzig, 1992.**

3.5.1 Thuringia in general

Essays on various aspects of Bach's time in Thuringian towns are found in
Landesarbeitsausschuss Thüringen. *Johann Sebastian Bach in Thüringen: Festgabe zum Gedenkjahr 1950,* edited by Heinrich Besseler and Günther Kraft. Weimar, 1950.

Der Landeskirchenrat der Evangelisch-Lutherischen Kirche in Thüringen, ed. *Bach in Thüringen: Gabe der Thüringer Kirche an das Thüringer Volk zum Bach-Gedenkjahr 1950.* Berlin, 1950.

3.5.2 Eisenach 1685–95

The most detailed studies of the Bach family in Eisenach and its musical life are
Claus Oefner. "Das Musikleben in Eisenach 1650–1750." Ph.D. diss. University of Halle-Wittenberg, 1975.

Claus Oefner. *Die Musikerfamilie Bach in Eisenach.* Eisenach, 1984.

Claus Oefner. "Eisenach zur Zeit des jungen Bach." *BJ* 71 (1985): 43–54.

3.5.3 Ohrdruf 1695–1700

The most significant literature on Ohrdruf and Bach's time there focuses on his older brother Johann Christoph, with whom he lived and studied, particularly
Hans-Joachim Schulze. "Johann Christoph Bach (1671 bis 1721), 'Organist und Schul Collega in Ohrdruf,' Johann Sebastian Bachs erster Lehrer." *BJ* 71 (1985): 55–81.

On the musical manuscript Bach compiled while living with his brother (the so-called moonlight manuscript), see
Robert Hill. "'Der Himmel weiss, wo diese Sachen hingekommen sind': reconstructing the lost keyboard notebooks of the young Bach and Handel." In *Bach, Handel, Scarlatti: tercentenary essays,* edited by Peter Williams, 161–72. Cambridge, 1985.

3.5.4 Lüneburg 1700–03

The most detailed writings on Bach in Lüneburg are

Gustav Fock. *Die Wahrheit über Bachs Aufenthalt in Lüneburg—Richtigstellungen zu Dr. E.W. Böhmes Schrift: Johann Sebastian Bach in Lüneburg.* Hamburg, 1949.

Gustav Fock. *Der junge Bach in Lüneburg, 1700 bis 1702.* Hamburg, 1950.

Of particular interest is the extensive music collection of the St. Michael School, where Bach was a student; the extent of his acquaintance with this collection is unknown. The inventory of manuscript music is transcribed in

Max Seiffert. "Die Chorbibliothek der St. Michaelisschule in Lüneburg zu Seb. Bach's Zeit." *Sammelbände der Internationalen Musik-Gesellschaft* 9, no. 4 (1908): 593–621.

The printed music is listed in

W. Junghans. "Johann Sebastian Bach als Schüler der Partikularschule zu St. Michaelis in Lüneburg, oder Lüneburg: eine Pflegstätte kirchlicher Musik." In *Programm des Johanneums zu Lüneburg: Ostern 1870.* Lüneburg, 1870.

On the collection in general, see

Friedhelm Krummacher. *Die Überlieferung der Choralbearbeitungen in der frühen evangelischen Kantate.* Berlin, 1965.

3.5.5 Weimar 1703

See *3.5.8 Weimar 1708–17.*

3.5.6 Arnstadt 1703–07

For essays on Bach's time in Arnstadt, as well as on other members of the family in that town, see

Karl Müller and Fritz Wiegand, eds. *Arnstädter Bachbuch: Johann Sebastian Bach und seine Verwandten in Arnstadt.* 2d. ed. Arnstadt, 1957.

For more recent details on Bach's time there, see

Markus Schiffner. "Johann Sebastian Bach in Arnstadt." Beiträge zur Bachforschung 4 (1985): 5–22.

3.5.7 *Mühlhausen 1707–08*

On Bach's time in Mühlhausen, see

Ernst Brinkmann. "Die Mühlhäuser Bache." In *Johann Sebastian Bach in Thüringen: Festgabe zum Gedenkjahr 1950,* edited by Heinrich Besseler and Günther Kraft, 220–28. Weimar, 1950.

3.5.8 *Weimar 1708–17*

The court of the dukedom of Saxe-Weimar had a fine musical establishment that had a great interest in modern Italian poetry and music. Bach held a minor position there for a few months in 1703; he returned in 1708 as a chamber musician and court organist and was promoted to *Konzertmeister* (leader of the orchestra) in 1714.

Many characters in this part of Bach's story have "Ernst" or "Johann" (or both) in their names; we offer here a brief summary of their identities. Duke Johann Ernst II (died 1683) had two sons who co-reigned as dukes of Saxe-Weimar. In 1703 Bach worked for the younger duke, Johann Ernst (died 1707). In 1708 he was hired by the elder, Wilhelm Ernst, who got on badly with his brother and with this brother's successor, Ernst August, who came of age in 1709. Ernst August's half-brother, Johann Ernst (the Ernst formally known as "Prince"), named after their father, was not a reigning duke, but he plays an important role in Bach's biography because he was a composer and because around 1713 he probably commissioned Bach to arrange for keyboard a series of modish Italian string concertos. Except during the last few months of his time in Weimar, Bach appears to have managed himself reasonably well with both sides of the family.

For an overview of Weimar's musical life during Bach's tenure there, see

Wolfgang Lidke. *Das Musikleben in Weimar von 1683 bis 1735.* Weimar, 1954.

Detailed reporting on the Weimar court archives is provided by

Reinhold Jauernig. "Johann Sebastian Bach in Weimar: neue Forschungsergebnisse aus Weimarer Quellen." In *Johann Sebastian Bach in Thüringen: Festgabe zum Gedenkjahr 1950*, edited by Heinrich Besseler and Günther Kraft, 49–105. Weimar, 1950.

For further interpretive discussion of the known documentation on Bach in Weimar, see

William Warren Cowdery. "The early vocal works of Johann Sebastian Bach: studies in style, scoring, and chronology." Ph.D. diss. Cornell University, 1989.

Bach's reasons for leaving Weimar for Köthen are discussed in

Andreas Glöckner. "Gründe für Johann Sebastian Bachs Weggang von Weimar." In *Bericht über die wissenschaftliche Konferenz zum V. internationalen Bachfest der DDR in Verbindung mit dem 60. Bachfest der Neuen Bachgesellschaft*, edited by Winfried Hoffmann and Armin Schneiderheinze, 137–43. Leipzig, 1988.

3.5.9 Köthen 1717–23

Anhalt-Köthen, where Bach's employer Prince Leopold ruled, was a rather insignificant principality among the German states. Owing to Leopold's extraordinary interest in music, its court had a first-rate orchestra. Bach was hired as *Kapellmeister* (director of the entire musical establishment).

The most extensive study of the city, though hard to come by, is

Oskar Hartung. *Geschichte der Stadt Cöthen bis zum Beginn des 19. Jahrhunderts.* Cöthen, 1900.

The classic work on Bach and Köthen is

Friedrich Smend. *Bach in Köthen.* Berlin, 1951. Translated by John Page and edited and revised by Stephen Daw as *Bach in Köthen.* St. Louis, 1985.

Smend actually had very little to say about Bach's position at the court or about the mostly instrumental works performed there. The book centers on Bach's vocal compositions, many of them later arranged by Bach with new librettos as church cantatas for the Leipzig liturgy. Smend was especially concerned to show that in Bach's Lutheranism, contrary to statements in traditional Bach scholarship, there was no "conflict" between secular and liturgical music.

To make up for the lack of information that readers might reasonably have expected to find in Smend's book, the English version provides an extra chapter summarizing previous research on the court, the musicians employed there, the palace itself, and the instrumental and vocal music Bach is known to have composed or arranged there; see

Stephen Daw. "Supplementary Material (Editorial)." In Friedrich Smend. *Bach in Köthen,* translated by John Page and edited and revised by Stephen Daw, 163–82. St. Louis, 1985.

41

For more recent work on Bach's time in Köthen, with important new information, see the extremely detailed study

> **Günther Hoppe. "Köthener politische, ökonomische und höfische Verhältnisse als Schaffensbedingungen Bachs (Teil 1)." Cöthener Bach-Hefte 4 (1986): 13–62.**

For an extensive bibliography on Bach and Köthen, see

> **Karl-Heinz Kresse and Günther Hoppe. "Bibliographie 'Der Köthener Bach: Leben und Werk.'" Cöthener Bach-Hefte 2 (1983): 32–50.**

Bach's reasons for leaving Köthen for Leipzig are discussed in

> **Ulrich Siegele. "Johann Sebastian Bachs und Fürst Leopolds Auffassungen über das Hofkapellmeisteramt." Cöthener Bach-Hefte 4 (1986): 9–12.**

3.5.10 Leipzig 1723–50

Because there has been considerable confusion over Bach's duties in Leipzig and his relationships with his employers, we thought some brief comments would be useful here.

Bach held a position as Cantor of the St. Thomas School (not Cantor of the St. Thomas Church, as writers in English often put it) and Musical Director of the city.

As *director musices* Bach provided music for civic occasions and for the city's churches, principally the St. Thomas and St. Nicholas Churches but several others as well. Bach's ensembles were made up of municipal musicians (Stadtpfeifer and Kunstgeiger), freelancers, and students from the St. Thomas School.

Traditionally, the cantor's job was to teach music and other subjects (for example, Latin) to students at the St. Thomas School. With reluctant permission from his employers in advance of his hiring, Bach was able to pay a student to take on these nonmusical duties soon after assuming his post.

In 1729 Bach took up the directorship of Leipzig's first *Collegium musicum* (the one founded by Georg Philipp Telemann), which was not a municipally supported institution. During his Leipzig tenure, Bach was also careful to keep or secure appointments as Kapellmeister (court composer) for nobility at Köthen, Weißenfels, and Dresden. His musical activities were thus extensive and wide-ranging.

Bach's various conflicts with authorities in Leipzig were not with the churches, as is often stated, or even, strictly speaking, with the Town Council as a whole, as has until recently been assumed.

The extremely illuminating essay

Ulrich Siegele. "Bach and the domestic politics of Electoral Saxony." In *The Cambridge companion to Bach,* **edited by John Butt, 17–34. Cambridge, 1997.**

shows that the Town Council consisted of two parties politically and culturally at odds: city-minded and court-minded councillors. This situation came about as part of the fundamental conflict of that time in Saxony, namely between the electoral ruler, who strove for absolute unlimited power, and the Estates, who strove to curb it. In Saxony, the Estates consisted primarily of two bodies, the nobility and the cities; with its established trade fairs, Leipzig was the leading city, and its deputies oversaw administrative duties for the Estates (that is, it was an especially important city within the state even though it had no court).

August the Strong, who ruled Saxony from 1694 to 1733, went to great lengths to consolidate and extend his power; in Leipzig, this included forcibly imposing mayoral appointments and packing the Town Council with men loyal to him. Thus when Bach applied for the job at Leipzig, he faced within the Council an absolutist faction who essentially wanted a *Kapellmeister* (a star composer and performer) and a city faction who wanted a traditional cantor (a schoolteacher). This meant not only that the search committee's proceedings would become protracted but also that inevitably there would be continual trouble ahead for the Council's unanimously agreed-upon compromise candidate, Bach.

For an excellent general introduction to the Leipzig of Bach's day, see
> **George B. Stauffer. "Leipzig: a cosmopolitan trade centre." In** *The late Baroque era: from the 1680s to 1740,* **edited by George J. Buelow, 254–95. Englewood Cliffs, 1994.**

The classic study of the city's musical life and Bach's time there is
> **Arnold Schering.** *Das Zeitalter Johann Sebastian Bachs und Johann Adam Hillers (von 1723 bis 1800).* **Vol. 3 of** *Johann Sebastian Bach und das Musikleben Leipzigs im 18. Jahrhundert: Musikgeschichte Leipzigs.* **Leipzig, 1941.**

For more on the issues surrounding Bach's hiring by the Leipzig Town Council, see
> **Ulrich Siegele. "Bachs Stellung in der Leipziger Kulturpolitik seiner Zeit."** *BJ* **69 (1983): 7–50; 70 (1984): 7–43; 72 (1986): 33–67.**

For a summary of those articles and for valuable new information on Leipzig's municipal and Saxony's electoral governments, see

Ulrich Siegele. "Bach and the domestic politics of Electoral Saxony." In *The Cambridge companion to Bach,* edited by John Butt, 17–34. Cambridge, 1997.

For details on Bach's musical test for his application, see
Christoph Wolff. "Bachs Leipziger Kantoratsprobe und die Aufführungsgeschichte der Kantate 'Du wahrer Gott und Davids Sohn' BWV 23." *BJ* 64 (1978): 78–94. Translated by Alfred Mann as "Bach's audition for the St. Thomas cantorate: the cantata 'Du wahrer Gott und Davids Sohn.'" In Wolff, *Bach: essays on his life and music,* 128–40. Cambridge, Mass., 1991.

Concerning Bach's *Schaffensrhythmus* (artistic productivity) at Leipzig, see
Rudolf Eller. "Gedanken über Bachs Leipziger Schaffensjahre." In *Eine Sammlung von Aufsätzen,* edited by Rudolf Eller and Hans-Joachim Schulze, 7–27. Bach-Studien 5. Leipzig, 1975. Translated by Stephen A. Crist as "Thoughts on Bach's Leipzig creative years." *Bach* 21, no. 2 (1990): 31–54.

For a history of the choirs at the St. Thomas School, see
Bernhard Knick. "Das Zeitalter Johann Sebastian Bachs." In *St. Thomas zu Leipzig, Schule und Chor: Stätte des Wirkens von Johann Sebastian Bach; Bilder und Dokumente zur Geschichte der Thomasschule und des Thomanerchores mit ihren zeitgeschichtlichen Beziehungen,* edited by Bernhard Knick, 135–262. Wiesbaden, 1963.

On the old music collection of the St. Thomas School, see
Arnold Schering. "Die alte Chorbibliothek der Thomasschule in Leipzig." *Archiv für Musikwissenschaft* 1 (1918–19): 275–88.

Bach studiously cited the regulations of the St. Thomas School in his disputes with the Leipzig Town Council. These ordinances have been reprinted in facsimile as

Hans-Joachim Schulze, ed. *Die Thomasschule Leipzig zur Zeit Johann Sebastian Bachs: Ordnungen und Gesetze 1634, 1723, 1733.* Leipzig, 1985.

One of these conflicts has generated much discussion in the secondary literature: the so-called Präfekten-Streit, over who had the right to appoint prefects (assistant directors of music students at the St. Thomas School); see
Paul S. Minear. "J.S. Bach and J.A. Ernesti: a case study in exegetical and theological conflict." In *Our common history as Christians: essays in*

honor of Albert C. Outler, edited by John Deschner et al., 131–55. New York, 1975.

The main documents of the Präfekten-Streit are printed conveniently next to each other in

Hans-Joachim Schulze, ed. *Johann Sebastian Bach: Leben und Werk in Dokumenten,* 47–57. Leipzig, 1975.

and in

BR, 137–49.

On Bach's direction of the Leipzig *Collegium musicum,* see

Werner Neumann. "Das 'Bachische *Collegium musicum.*'" *BJ* 47 (1960): 5–27. Reprinted in *Johann Sebastian Bach,* edited by Walter Blankenburg, 384–415. Wege der Forschung 170. Darmstadt, 1970.

Herbert R. Pankratz. "J.S. Bach and his Leipzig *Collegium musicum.*" *Musical Quarterly* 69 (1983): 323–53.

On the life of the churches in Leipzig and Bach's relationship to them, see

Günther Stiller. *Johann Sebastian Bach und das Leipziger gottesdienst-liche Leben seiner Zeit.* Cassel, 1970. Translated by Herbert J.A. Bouman et al. and edited by Robin A. Leaver as *Johann Sebastian Bach and liturgical life in Leipzig.* St. Louis, 1984.

The architecture of the St. Thomas Church is described in

Herbert Stiehl. *Das Innere der Thomaskirche zur Amtszeit Johann Sebastian Bachs.* Beiträge zur Bachforschung 3. Leipzig, 1984.

During some years, Bach was responsible for performing church cantatas in the University church; see

Reinhard Szeskus. "Bach und die Leipziger Universitätsmusik." *Beiträge zur Musikwissenschaft* 32 (1990): 161–70. Also in *Alte Musik als ästhetische Gegenwart—Bach, Händel, Schütz: Bericht über den internationalen musikwissenschaftlichen Kongreß Stuttgart 1985,* edited by Dietrich Berke and Dorothee Hanemann, vol. 1: 405–12. Cassel, 1987.

For extensive discussion of the New Church and its relationship to the churches whose music Bach directed, see

Andreas Glöckner. *Die Musikpflege an der Leipziger Neukirche zur Zeit Johann Sebastian Bachs.* Beiträge zur Bachforschung 8. Leipzig, 1990.

Concerning the Town Council's search for Bach's successor, see

Arnold Schering. *Das Zeitalter Johann Sebastian Bachs und Johann Adam Hillers (von 1723 bis 1800).* Vol. 3 of *Johann Sebastian Bach und das Musikleben Leipzigs im 18. Jahrhundert: Musikgeschichte Leipzigs,* 326–28. Leipzig, 1941.

3.5.11 Other places with Bach connections

Dresden

Dresden was the court seat of the Saxon electorate. It had one of the finest musical establishments in the German states. For both of these reasons, Bach continually sought contact there. Bach made several visits, wrote secular cantatas for the royal family (BWV 193a, 205a, 206, 207a, 208a, 213–215, Anh. I 9, 11–13), dedicated the *Missa* BWV 232^{I} to the elector in 1733, and secured a court title in 1736.

For a general introduction to the Dresden of Bach's day and its musical culture, see

George J. Buelow. "Dresden in the age of absolutism." In *The late Baroque era: from the 1680s to 1740*, edited by George J. Buelow, 216–29. Englewood Cliffs, 1994.

The classic study of the history of the musical life there is

Moritz Fürstenau. *Zur Geschichte der Musik und des Theaters am Hofe zu Dresden.* 2 vols. Dresden, 1861–62.

For more recent information, see

Irmgard Becker-Glauch. *Die Bedeutung der Musik für die Dresdener Hoffeste bis in die Zeit Augusts des Starken.* Cassel, 1951.

More recent information on church music at the court is provided in

Wolfgang Horn. *Die Dresdener Hofkirchenmusik 1720–1745: Studien zu ihren Voraussetzungen und ihrem Repertoire.* Cassel, 1987.

For more recent research on the court's musical scene, particularly in Bach's day, see also

Ortrun Landmann. "The Dresden Hofkapelle during the lifetime of Johann Sebastian Bach." *Early Music* 17 (1989): 17–30.

On Bach's musical indebtedness to Dresden repertory, see

Robert L. Marshall. "Bach the progressive: observations on his later works." *Musical Quarterly* 62 (1976): 313–57. Rev. in his *The music of Johann Sebastian Bach: the sources, the style, the significance,* 23–58. New York, 1989.

For an older bibliography on Bach and Dresden, see
> **Werner Neumann and Rudolf Eller.** "Bach und Dresden: eine Bibliographie." In *43. Deutsches Bach-Fest der Neuen Bachgesellschaft 6.–9. Dezember in Dresden—Bachfestbuch*, 40–43. Dresden, 1968.

Berlin

Berlin was the court seat of Prussia, one of the two most powerful German states in the eighteenth century. Bach dedicated the *Brandenburg Concertos* to the Margrave of Brandenburg, Christian Ludwig of Berlin. Bach's connections to the city intensified again in the 1740s, when several of his students and his son Carl Philipp Emanuel joined the royal musical establishment there. In 1747 he dedicated the *Musical Offering* BWV 1079 to King Frederick the Great, after having performed at court in Potsdam.

For an introduction to musical culture of the Berlin of Bach's day, see
> **Curt Sachs.** *Musik und Oper am kurbrandenburgischen Hof.* Berlin, 1910.

On musical life under Frederick the Great, see
> **Ernest Eugene Helm.** *Music at the court of Frederick the Great.* Norman, 1960.

On Bach's connections with the city, see
> **Hans Theodore David.** *J.S. Bach's Musical Offering: history, interpretation, analysis*, 3–15. New York, 1945.

> **Andreas Holschneider.** "Johann Sebastian Bach in Berlin." In *Preußen, Dein Spree-Athen: Beiträge zu Literatur, Theater und Musik in Berlin*, edited by Hellmut Kühn, 135–45. Reinbeck bei Hamburg, 1981.

Weißenfels

Weißenfels was the seat of a dukedom where Bach's second wife, Anna Magdalena, had been a singer (her father was a court trumpeter). Bach wrote the cantatas BWV 208 and 249a for Duke Christian of Weißenfels, and he secured a court title in the late 1720s.

The classic study of the history of the musical scene in Weißenfels is
> **Arno Werner.** *Städtische und fürstliche Musikpflege in Weissenfels bis zum Ende des 18. Jahrhunderts.* Leipzig, 1911.

For more recent information on Weißenfels in Bach's time, see also
> **Eva-Maria Ranft.** "Zum Personalbestand der Weißenfelser Hofkapelle." *Beiträge zur Bachforschung* 6 (1987): 5–36.

On Bach's musical and titular connections there, see
> Klaus Hofmann. "Johann Sebastian Bachs Kantate 'Jauchzet Gott in allen Landen' BWV 51: Überlegungen zu Entstehung und ursprünglicher Bestimmung." *BJ* 75 (1989): 43–54.

On Bach's familial connections there, see
> Adolf Schmiedecke. "Johann Sebastian Bachs Verwandte in Weißenfels." *Die Musikforschung* 14 (1961): 195–200.

> Eva-Maria Ranft. "Neues über die Weißenfelser Verwandtschaft Anna Magdalena Bachs." *BJ* 73 (1987): 169–71.

Lübeck

For information on Bach's extended trip to Lübeck, see
> Kerala J. Snyder. "To Lübeck in the steps of J.S. Bach." *Musical Times* 127 (1986): 672–77. Reprinted in *Bach* 20, no. 2 (1989): 38–48.

> Gottfried Simpfendörfer. "Wo lernte Johann Sebastian Bach die Schriften Heinrich Müllers kennen?" *BJ* 79 (1993): 205–11.

Halle

Concerning Bach's application for a position at Halle, see
> Peter Wollny. "Bachs Bewerbung um die Organistenstelle an der Marienkirche zu Halle und ihr Kontext." *BJ* 80 (1994): 25–39.

> Alfred Dürr. "Zu Johann Sebastian Bachs Hallenser Probestück von 1713." *BJ* 81 (1995): 183–84.

Hamburg

Concerning Bach's application for a position at Hamburg, see
> Joachim Kremer. "Die Organistenstelle an St. Jakobi in Hamburg: eine 'convenable station' für Johann Sebastian Bach?" *BJ* 79 (1993): 217–22.

4

Bach's world

4.1 Bach's teaching and students

4.1.1 Bach's teaching

The principal reports on Bach's teaching are the following:

Carl Philipp Emanuel Bach's letter to Johann Nikolaus Forkel, 13 January 1775 [*Dok* III/803; *BR,* 279].

This material is related with additional detail in chapter 7 (*BR,* 327–33) of
Johann Nikolaus Forkel. *Ueber Johann Sebastian Bachs Leben, Kunst und Kunstwerke: für patriotische Verehrer echter musikalischer Kunst.* **Leipzig, 1802, and reprints.**

Johann Philipp Kirnberger's comments in
Johann Philipp Kirnberger. *Gedanken über die verschiedenen Lehrarten.* **Berlin, 1782. [*Dok* III/867; *BR,* 262]**

Ernst Ludwig Gerber's entry for his father Heinrich Nicolaus Gerber in
Ernst Ludwig Gerber. *Historisch-Biographisches Lexicon der Tonkünstler.* **2 vols. Leipzig, 1790. [*Dok* III/950; *BR,* 263–65]**

On Gerber and Bach see
Alfred Dürr. "Heinrich Nicolaus Gerber als Schüler Bachs." *BJ* 64 (1978): 7–18, at 9–10.

Johann Friedrich Agricola's comments in
Johann Friedrich Agricola. *Allgemeine deutsche Bibliothek* 22:243. **Berlin and Stettin, 1774. [*Dok* III/796]**

Bach's basso continuo rules, based on those of Friedrich Erhard Niedt, were recorded in manuscript (Brussels, Bibliothèque du Conservatoire Royal de Musique, Ms no. 27.224) by Carl August Thieme ("Vorschriften und Grundsätze zum vierstimmigen Spielen des General-Bass oder Accompagnement"). [*Dok* II/433 (title page only); *BR*, 392–98] Complete transcription and commentary in

> **Pamela L. Poulin, transl.** *J.S. Bach's precepts and principles for playing the thorough-bass or accompanying in four parts: Leipzig, 1738.* Oxford, 1994. [with facsimile]

On the identification of Thieme as the copyist see

> **Hans-Joachim Schulze.** *Studien zur Bach-Überlieferung im 18. Jahrhundert*, 125–27. Leipzig, 1984.

Bach's music anthologies for members of his family should also be considered pedagogical documents. Surviving are one for Wilhelm Friedemann Bach (edited in NBA V/5) and two for Anna Magdalena Bach (edited in NBA V/4). See also

> **Robert L. Marshall.** "The notebooks for Wilhelm Friedemann and Anna Magdalena Bach: some biographical lessons." In *Essays in musicology: a tribute to Alvin Johnson*, edited by Lewis Lockwood and Edward Roesner, 192–200. Philadelphia, 1990.

On Bach's teaching in general see

> **Alfred Mann.** *Theory and practice: the great composer as student and teacher.* New York, 1987.

4.1.2 Bach's students

The only systematic list of Bach's students is old but still a useful starting point:

> **Hans Löffler.** "Die Schüler Joh. Seb. Bachs." *BJ* 40 (1953): 5–28.

Here are several surveys of compositions by Bach's students:

> **Reinhold Sietz.** "Die Orgelkompositionen des Schülerkreises um Johann Sebastian Bach." *BJ* 32 (1935): 33–96.

> **Hermann Max.** "Verwandtes im Werk Bach, seiner Schüler und Söhne." In *Johann Sebastian Bachs Spätwerk und dessen Umfeld: Perspektiven und Probleme*, edited by Christoph Wolff, 117–47. Cassel, 1988.

> **Ulrich Matyl.** *Die Choralbearbeitungen der Schüler Johann Sebastian Bachs.* Cassel, 1996.

Bach's most important students (apart from his children, on whom see *3.1.3 Children*) are listed here, together with literature about their studies with Bach. For each of the students, see also the relevant materials in *Dok.* For literature on students and family members as copyists, see *5.1.3 Bach's copyists.*

Johann Christoph Altnickol

Walter Emery. "Altnikol, Johann Christoph." *New Grove.*

Johann Friedrich Doles

Daniel R. Melamed. "J.F. Doles's setting of a Picander libretto and J.S. Bach's teaching of vocal composition." *Journal of Musicology* 14 (1996): 453–74.

Heinrich Nicolaus Gerber

Alfred Dürr. "Heinrich Nicolaus Gerber als Schüler Bachs." *BJ* 64 (1978): 7–18.

Johann Gottlieb Goldberg

Alfred Dürr. "Johann Gottlieb Goldberg und die Triosonate BWV 1037." *BJ* 40 (1953): 51–80.

Alfred Dürr, ed. *Gottfried Kirchhoff . . . und Johann Gottlieb Goldberg . . . : Kirchenkantaten.* Das Erbe deutscher Musik 35. Cassel, 1957.

Gottfried August Homilius

Hans John. *Der Dresdner Kreuzkantor und Bach-Schüler Gottfried August Homilius: ein Beitrag zur Musikgeschichte Dresdens im 18. Jahrhundert.* Tutzing, 1980.

Johann Peter Kellner

It is not known for certain whether Kellner was a Bach student. In any event, he was an important transmitter of Bach's instrumental music.

Russell Stinson. *The Bach manuscripts of Johann Peter Kellner and his circle: a case study in reception history.* Durham, N.C., 1989.

Johann Philipp Kirnberger

Siegfried Borris[-Zuckermann]. *Kirnbergers Leben und Werk und seine Bedeutung im Berliner Musikkreis um 1750.* Cassel, 1933.

Ruth Engelhardt. "Untersuchungen über Einflüsse Johann Sebastian Bachs auf das theoretische und praktischer Wirken seines Schülers Johann Philipp Kirnberger." Ph.D. diss. University of Erlangen-Nürnberg, 1974.

Johann Christoph Kittel

Albert Dreetz. *Johann Christian Kittel: der letzte Bach-Schüler.* Berlin, 1932.

Philipp David Kräuter

Franz Krautwurst. "Der Augsburger Bach-Schüler Philipp David Kräuter." *Augsburger Jahrbuch für Musikwissenschaft 1990,* 31–52. Tutzing, 1990.

Johann Ludwig Krebs

Karl Tittel. "Vom 'einzigen Krebs in meinem Bach': Johann Ludwig Krebs (1713–1780) als Bachschüler und Orgelkomponist." *Musik und Kirche* 46 (1976): 172–81.

Lorenz Christoph Mizler

Franz Wöhlke. *Lorenz Christoph Mizler: ein Beitrag zur musikalischen Gelehrtengeschichte des 18. Jahrhunderts.* Würzburg-Aumühle, 1940.

Johann Gottfried Müthel

Erwin Kemmler. *Johann Gottfried Müthel (1728–1788) und das nordostdeutsche Musikleben seiner Zeit.* Marburg, 1970.

[Johann] Christoph Nichelmann

Hans-Joachim Schulze. *Studien zur Bach-Überlieferung im 18. Jahrhundert,* 130–45. Leipzig, 1984.

Johann Adolph Scheibe

Russell Stinson. "The 'critischer musikus' as keyboard transcriber? Scheibe, Bach, and Vivaldi." *Journal of Musicological Research* 9 (1990): 255–71.

Georg Gottfried Wagner

Hans-Joachim Schulze. "Johann Sebastian Bach und Georg Gottfried Wagner—neue Dokumente." Bach-Studien 5 (1975): 147–54.

4.2 Bach's library

A list of religious books from Bach's library, written up after Bach's death, is found in chapter 12 of
> "*Specificatio* der Verlaßenschafft des am 28. *July.* 1750 seelig verstorbenen Herrn Johann *Sebastian* Bachs." Transcribed in *Dok* II/627. Translated in *BR,* 191–97.

There is no mention here of Bach's books on other subjects. Bach's books on music had no doubt already been passed on to his sons before this point.

A catalogue and study of this list of religious books appears in
> **Robin A. Leaver.** *Bachs theologische Bibliothek: eine kritische Bibliographie / Bach's theological library: a critical bibliography.* Neuhausen-Stuttgart, 1983.

For further useful information and minor corrections, see
> **Johannes Wallmann.** "Johann Sebastian Bach und die 'Geistlichen Bücher' seiner Bibliothek." *Pietismus und Neuzeit* 12 (1986): 162–81.

To determine which writings of Martin Luther were printed in the volumes that Bach owned, consult Leaver's bibliography together with
> **Kurt Aland.** *Hilfsbuch zum Lutherstudium.* Rev. ed. Witten, 1970.

The only known surviving religious book from Bach's library itself is
> **Abraham Calov.** *Die heilige Bibel nach S. Herrn D. Martini Lutheri Deutscher Dolmetschung und Erklärung.* Wittenberg, 1681–82.

This Bible contains a considerable number of marginal comments and underlinings that have been scientifically identified as coming from Bach's pen. Facsimiles of each of these passages and translations are provided in
> **Howard H. Cox, ed.** *The Calov Bible of J.S. Bach.* Ann Arbor, 1985.

Facsimiles of Bach's marginal comments and a study of them are found in
> **Robin A. Leaver.** *J.S. Bach and scripture: glosses from the Calov Bible Commentary.* St. Louis, 1985.

See also
> **Renate Steiger.** "Lesespuren—Lesefrüchte: zu J.S. Bachs Umgang mit seiner Bibliothek." *Musik und Kirche* 63 (1993): 77–80.

For some information on the books about music that were or might have been in Bach's personal library, see
> **Stanley Godman.** "Bachs Bibliothek: die noch vorhandenen Handexemplare." *Musica* 10 (1956): 756–61.

Ulrich Leisinger. "Die 'Bachsche Auction' von 1789." *BJ* 77 (1991): 97–126.

A detailed catalog and study of the music (by other composers) found in Bach's personal library appears in
Kirsten Beißwenger. *Johann Sebastian Bachs Notenbibliothek.* Cassel, 1992.

On the musical significance of Bach's library, see *10.2 Bach and the music of other composers.*

4.3 Liturgical context

4.3.1 The liturgical year

The church calendar is the context for the performance of much of Bach's sacred music. An extremely useful tool in understanding the calendar is the following, which contains a perpetual liturgical calendar and a detailed glossary of alternative names for the feasts of the year.

Hermann Grotefend. *Handbuch der historischen Chronologie des deutschen Mittelalters und der Neuzeit.* **Hannover, 1872.**

For the student of Bach's church music, one particularly important aspect of the calendar was the assignment of biblical texts for each Sunday and feast. Here is a summary table of the liturgical year and the assigned texts. The first part of the table presents the moveable feasts and Sundays, the second part, the fixed feast days. Note that not all days recur each liturgical year; the number of Sundays after Christmas (0–1), New Year's Day (0–1), Epiphany (3–6), and Trinity (22–27) vary, depending mostly on when Easter falls. Bracketed feasts are those that may or may not be present in a given year. The three principal feasts—Christmas, Easter, and Pentecost—are celebrated for three days each.

The five rightmost columns in the table list Bach's church cantatas for each feast: those composed before his move to Leipzig in 1723 (Pre-L), those from Bach's first three Leipzig cycles (I, II, III), and others. Note that the assignment of cantatas to cycles is a matter of interpretation; see *7.3.1 Cantatas.*

The liturgical calendar

Feast / Sunday		[For the] Epistle	Gospel	Pre-L	I	II	III	Other
1. Advent	1st Sun in Advent	Rom 13:11–14	Matt 21:1–9	61	61	62		36
2. Advent	2d Sun in Advent	Rom 15:4–13	Luke 21:25–36	70a				
3. Advent	3d Sun in Advent	1 Cor 4:1–5	Matt 11:2–10	186a				
4. Advent	4th Sun in Advent	Phil 4:4–7	John 1:19–28	132, 147a				
1. Weihnachtstag	Christmas Day	Titus 2:1–14	Luke 2:1–14	63	63	91	110	197a
2. Weihnachtstag	2d Day of Christmas	I: Titus 3:4–7; II: Acts 6:8–9 and 7:54–59	I: Luke 2:15–20; II: Matt 23:34–9		40	121	57	
3. Weihnachtstag	3d Day of Christmas	I: Heb 1:1–14; II: 1 John 1:1–10	I: John 1:1–14; II: John 21:20–24		64	133	151	
[Sonntag nach Weihnachten	Sun aft Christmas]	Gal 4:1–7	Luke 2:33–40	152		122	28	
Neujahr	New Year's Day	Gal 3:23–9	Luke 2:21		190	41	16	171
[Sonntag nach Neujahr	Sun aft New Year's Day]	1 Pet 4:12–19	Matt 2:13–23		153		58	

(cont'd)

The liturgical calendar, *continued*

Feast / Sunday		[For the] Epistle	Gospel	Pre-L	I	II	III	Other
Epiphanias	Epiphany	Isa 60:1–6	Matt 2:1–12		65	123		
1. Sonntag nach Epiphanias	1st Sun aft Epiphany	Rom 12:1–6	Luke 2:41–52		154	124	32	
2. Sonntag nach Epiphanias	2d Sun aft Epiphany	Rom 12:6–16	John 2:1–11	155	155	3	13	
3. Sonntag nach Epiphanias	3d Sun aft Epiphany	Rom 12:17–21	Matt 8:1–13		73	111	72	156
[4. Sonntag nach Epiphanias	4th Sun aft Epiphany]	Rom 13:8–10	Matt 8:23–7		81			14
[5. Sonntag nach Epiphanias	5th Sun aft Epiphany]	Col 3:12–17	Matt 13:24–30					
[6. Sonntag nach Epiphanias	6th Sun aft Epiphany]	1 Thess 1:2–10	Matt 13:31–5					
Septuagisimae	3d Sun bef Lent	1 Cor 9:24–10:5	Matt 20:1–16		144	92	84	
Sexagesimae	2d Sun bef Lent	2 Cor 11:19–12:9	Luke 8:4–15	18	181	126		
Estomihi [= Quinquagesimae]	Sun bef Lent	1 Cor 13:1–13	Luke 18:31–48	23, 22	23, 22	127		159
Invocavit	1st Sun in Lent	2 Cor 6:1–10	Matt 4:1–11					
Reminiscere	2d Sun in Lent	1 Thess 4:1–7	Matt 17:1–9					
Oculi	3d Sun in Lent	Eph 5:1–9	Luke 11:14–28	54, 80a				

Läetare	4th Sun in Lent	Gal 4:22–31	John 6:1–15					
Judica	5th Sun in Lent	Heb 9:11–15	John 8:46–59					BC A58
Palmarum	Palm Sun	I: Phil 2:5–11; II: 1 Cor 11:23–32	Matt 21:1–9	182				145, 158
1. Ostertag	Easter Sun	1 Cor 5:6–8	Mark 16:1–8	4, 31	4, 31	4		
2. Ostertag	Easter Monday	Acts 10:34–43	Luke 24:13–35		66	6		
3. Ostertag	Easter Tuesday	Acts 13:26–47	Luke 24:36–47		134			
Quasimodogeniti	1st Sun aft Easter	1 John 5:4–10	John 20:19–31		67	42		
Misericordias Domini	2d Sun aft Easter	1 Pet 2:21–5	John 10:12–16		104	85		112
Jubilate	3d Sun aft Easter	1 Pet 2:11–20	John 16:16–23	12	12	103	146	
Cantate	4th Sun aft Easter	James 1:17–21	John 16:5–15		166	108		
Rogate	5th Sun aft Easter	James 1:22–7	John 16:23–30		86	87		
Himmelfahrt	Ascension	Acts 1:1–11	Mark 16:14–20		37	128	43	
Exaudi	Sun aft Ascension	1 Pet 4:8–11	John 15:26–16:4		44	183		
1. Pfingsttag	Pentecost Sun	Acts 2:1–13	John 14:23–31	172	172, 59	74		34

(cont'd)

The liturgical calendar, *continued*

Feast / Sunday		[For the] Epistle	Gospel	Pre-L	I	II	III	Other
2. Pfingsttag	Pentecost Monday	Acts 10:42–8	John 3:16–21		173	68		174
3. Pfingsttag	Pentecost Tuesday	Acts 8:14–17	John 10:1–11		184	175		
Trinitatis	Trinity	Rom 11:33–6	John 3:1–15	165	194	176	129	
1. Sonntag nach Trinitatis	1st Sun aft Trinity	1 John 4:16–21	Luke 16:19–31		75	20	39	
2. Sonntag nach Trinitatis	2d Sun aft Trinity	1 John 3:13–18	Luke 14:16–24		76	2		
3. Sonntag nach Trinitatis	3d Sun aft Trinity	1 Pet 5:6–11	Luke 15:1–10	21	21	135		
4. Sonntag nach Trinitatis	4th Sun aft Trinity	Rom 8:18–23	Luke 6:36–42	185	185, 24			177
5. Sonntag nach Trinitatis	5th Sun aft Trinity	1 Pet 3:8–15	Luke 5:1–11			93	88	
6. Sonntag nach Trinitatis	6th Sun aft Trinity	Rom 6:3–11	Matt 5:20–6				170	9
7. Sonntag nach Trinitatis	7th Sun aft Trinity	Rom 6:19–23	Mark 8:1–9		186	107	187	
8. Sonntag nach Trinitatis	8th Sun aft Trinity	Rom 8:12–17	Matt 7:15–23		136	178	45	
9. Sonntag nach Trinitatis	9th Sun aft Trinity	1 Cor 10:6–13	Luke 16:1–9		105	94	168	
10. Sonntag nach Trinitatis	10th Sun aft Trinity	1 Cor 12:1–11	Luke 19:41–8		46	101	102	
11. Sonntag nach Trinitatis	11th Sun aft Trinity	1 Cor 15:1–10	Luke 18:9–14	199	179, 199	113		
12. Sonntag nach Trinitatis	12th Sun aft Trinity	2 Cor 3:4–11	Mark 7:31–7		69a	137	35	

German	English	Epistle		Gospel				
13. Sonntag nach Trinitatis	13th Sun aft Trinity	Gal 3:15–22		Luke 10:23–37	77	33	164	
14. Sonntag nach Trinitatis	14th Sun aft Trinity	Gal 5:16–24		Luke 17:11–19	25	78	17	
15. Sonntag nach Trinitatis	15th Sun aft Trinity	Gal 5:25–6:10		Matt 6:24–34	138	99		51
16. Sonntag nach Trinitatis	16th Sun aft Trinity	Eph 3:13–21	161	Luke 7:11–17	95	8	27	
17. Sonntag nach Trinitatis	17th Sun aft Trinity	Eph 4:1–6		Luke 14:1–11	148	114	47	
18. Sonntag nach Trinitatis	18th Sun aft Trinity	1 Cor 1:4–9		Matt 22:34–46		96	169	
19. Sonntag nach Trinitatis	19th Sun aft Trinity	Eph 4:22–8		Matt 9:1–8	48	5	56	
20. Sonntag nach Trinitatis	20th Sun aft Trinity	Eph 5:15–21	162	Matt 22:1–14	162	180	49	
21. Sonntag nach Trinitatis	21st Sun aft Trinity	Eph 6:10–17		John 4:47–54	109	38	98	188
22. Sonntag nach Trinitatis	22d Sun aft Trinity	Phil 1:3–11		Matt 18:23–35	89	115	55	
23. Sonntag nach Trinitatis	[23d Sun aft Trinity]	Phil 3:17–21	163	Matt 22:15–22		139	52	
24. Sonntag nach Trinitatis	[24th Sun aft Trinity]	Col 1:9–14		Matt 9:18–26	60	26		
25. Sonntag nach Trinitatis	[25th Sun aft Trinity]	1 Thess 4:13–18		Matt 24:15–28	90	116		
26. Sonntag nach Trinitatis	[26th Sun aft Trinity]	2 Pet 3:3–13		Matt 25:31–46	70			
27. Sonntag nach Trinitatis	[27th Sun aft Trinity]	1 Thess 5:1–11		Matt 25:1–13				140
Mariae Reinigung	Purification (2 Feb)	Mal 3:1–4		Luke 2:22–32	83	125	82	157

(cont'd)

The liturgical calendar, *continued*

Feast / Sunday		[For the] Epistle	Gospel	Pre-L	I	II	III	Other
Mariae Verkündigung	Annunciation (25 March)	Isa 7:10–16	Luke 1:26–38		182	1		
Johannistag	St. John (24 June)	Isa 40:1–5	Luke 1:57–80		167	7		30
Mariae Heimsuchung	Visitation (2 July)	Isa 11:1–5	Luke 1:39–56		147	10		
Michaelistag	St. Michael (29 Sept)	Rev 12:7–12	Matt 18:1–11			130	19	149
Reformationsfest	Reformation Day (31 Oct)	2 Thess 2:3–8	Rev 14:6–8				79	80

4.3.2 The liturgy

Here we present basic literature on the liturgy in Bach's time. (For broader theological concerns, see *11.2 Theological studies*.) Liturgical practice is best documented in and has been most studied for Leipzig.

Bach himself twice recorded the order of service for the first Sunday in Advent; see *Dok* I/178 (*BR,* 70) and *Dok* I/181.

The most complete study of Leipzig liturgical practice is

Günther Stiller. *Johann Sebastian Bach und das Leipziger gottesdienstliche Leben seiner Zeit.* **Cassel, 1970. Translated by Herbert J.A. Bouman et al. and edited by Robin A. Leaver as** *Johann Sebastian Bach and liturgical life in Leipzig.* **St. Louis, 1984.**

On Bach's music in the context of the liturgy, see

Robin A. Leaver. "The mature vocal works and their theological and liturgical context." In *The Cambridge companion to Bach,* **edited by John Butt, 86–122. Cambridge, 1997.**

A week-by-week reconstruction of the liturgy—in need of revision but still extremely useful—is

Charles Sanford Terry. *Joh. Seb. Bach: cantata texts, sacred and secular, with a reconstruction of the Leipzig liturgy of his period.* **London, 1926.**

Many matters concerning music and the liturgy are discussed in

Arnold Schering. *Johann Sebastian Bachs Leipziger Kirchenmusik: Studien und Wege zu ihrer Erkenntnis.* **2d ed. Leipzig, 1954.**

For pictures and documents connected with Bach and the liturgy, see

Martin Petzoldt. *Ehre sei dir Gott gesungen: Bilder und Texte zu Bachs Leben als Christ und seinem Wirken für die Kirche.* **2d ed. Göttingen, 1990.**

The hymnals—which include some liturgical music—most relevant to the places where Bach composed his church music are

Auserlesenes Weinmarisches [sic] *Gesangbuch.* **Weimar, 1681.**

Neu-auffgelegtes Dreßdnisches Gesang-Buch. **Dresden and Leipzig, 1707 and later editions.**

Gottfried Vopelius. *Neu Leipziger Gesangbuch.* **Leipzig, 1682 and later editions.**

On the Vopelius hymnal, see

Jürgen Grimm. *Das Neu Leipziger Gesangbuch des Gottfried Vopelius (Leipzig 1682): Untersuchungen zur Klärung seiner geschichtlichen Stellung.* Berlin, 1969.

For an overview on Bach and hymnody, see

Robin A. Leaver. "Bach, hymns and hymnbooks." *The Hymn* 36, no. 4 (1985): 7–13.

For literature on hymns, see *7.3.6 Four-part chorales.*

5

Sources and transmission

A great deal of Bach scholarship, especially in the last fifty years, has been devoted to the study of the sources of his music. Source studies seek to answer questions about a work's authenticity, date, genesis, musical text, performance history and reception by a close examination of the manuscripts and original editions that preserve it.

5.1 Source study

5.1.1 Sources and facsimiles

The most comprehensive list of sources for an individual work will always be found in the critical commentary to the appropriate volume of the Neue Bach-Ausgabe (see *6.2.3 Neue Bach-Ausgabe*). A compact and detailed summary of the most important sources for a work can be found in its entry in the BC, and less comprehensively, in the BWV (see *1.1 Basic reference tools*).

> Facsimiles of autograph sources are listed comprehensively in
> **Yoshitake Kobayashi. *Die Notenschrift Johann Sebastian Bachs: Dokumentation ihrer Entwicklung,* 217–20. NBA ix/2. Cassel, 1989.**

For references to complete or partial reproductions of an individual work, see its entry in the BC.

> The surviving original parts for Bach's vocal music are nicely summarized in Appendix A of
> **Laurence Dreyfus. *Bach's continuo group: players and practices in his vocal works.* Cambridge, Mass., 1987.**

5.1.2 J.S. Bach's handwriting

Bach studies have relied heavily on the detailed examination of Bach's

63

handwriting and its changes over his life. The principal areas of research concern Bach's handwriting as a clue to the dates of sources and compositions, and the character of Bach's handwriting in particular manuscripts (working script versus fair copy hand) as evidence of whether he was composing a new work or copying an older one.

The two fundamental studies of Bach's handwriting are the following (the second contains a chronology of Bach's Leipzig works):

Georg von Dadelsen. *Bemerkungen zur Handschrift Johann Sebastian Bachs, seiner Familie und seines Kreises.* **Tübinger Bach-Studien 1. Trossingen, 1957.**

Georg von Dadelsen. *Beiträge zur Chronologie der Werke Johann Sebastian Bachs.* **Tübinger Bach-Studien 4/5. Trossingen, 1958.**

Bach's early handwriting is investigated in

Yoshitake Kobayashi. "Quellenkundliche Überlegungen zur Chronologie der Weimarer Vokalwerke Bachs." In *Das Frühwerk Johann Sebastian Bachs: Kolloquium veranstaltet vom Institut für Musikwissenschaft der Universität Rostock 11.–13. September 1990,* **edited by Karl Heller and Hans-Joachim Schulze, 290–310. Cologne, 1995.**

Bach's late handwriting is investigated in detail in the following study, which includes a chronology of Bach's scores and performing material from the last fifteen years of his life.

Yoshitake Kobayashi. "Zur Chronologie der Spätwerke Johann Sebastian Bachs: Kompositions- und Aufführungstätigkeit von 1736 bis 1750." *BJ* **74 (1988): 7–72.**

There are several useful collections of facsimiles of Bach's handwriting. The most complete is

Yoshitake Kobayashi. *Die Notenschrift Johann Sebastian Bachs: Dokumentation ihrer Entwicklung.* **NBA ix/2. Cassel, 1989.**

This volume contains 150 reproductions in chronological order, with detailed commentary, an index of Bach's autographs and copies of other composers' music, and a list of published facsimiles.

Joh. Seb. Bach's Handschrift in zeitlich geordneten Nachbildungen. **BG 44. Leipzig, 1895.**

Alfred Dürr. *Johann Sebastian Bach: seine Handschrift—Abbild seines Schaffens.* **Wiesbaden, 1984.**

These two volumes, of which the second is an updated and annotated reprint of the first, also provide a broad sample of Bach's handwriting.

Bach's use of different rastrals (tools for putting staff lines on paper) is investigated in

> **Christoph Wolff. "Die Rastrierungen in den Originalhandschriften Joh. Seb. Bachs und ihre Bedeutung für die diplomatische Quellenkritik." In** *Festschrift für Friedrich Smend zum 70. Geburtstag,* **80–92. Berlin, 1963.**

5.1.3 Bach's copyists

The distinguishing and identification of the many copyists who assisted J.S. Bach has been an essential tool in Bach studies. A catalogue of these copyists and their work is planned as a supplemental volume to the NBA. The indexes of the BC will also be a point of access to copyists and their work. Note that most of the copyists were sorted out and identified with sigla before their names were known, so many important studies refer to them only as "Anonymous __."

Best studied are Bach family members and the Leipzig students and assistants who helped in the performance of his church compositions. Their handwritings are systematically examined in

> **Georg von Dadelsen.** *Bemerkungen zur Handschrift Johann Sebastian Bachs, seiner Familie und seines Kreises.* **Tübinger Bach-Studien 1. Trossingen, 1957.**

> **Alfred Dürr.** *Zur Chronologie der Leipziger Vokalwerke J.S. Bachs.* **2d ed. Cassel, 1976.**

Dadelsen assigned sigla to four important copyists (Anonymous 1–4). Dürr assigned sigla to principal copyists (Hauptkop. A–H, of whom A, B, C and H are the same as Dadelsen's Anonymous 3, 1, 2, and 4, respectively) and to secondary scribes (Anon. Ia–Iq, IIa–IIh, etc.); the roman numerals in their sigla refer to the Jahrgang (cantata cycle) on which they worked. Dürr's study includes a list of copyists and their work.

Many anonymous copyists are identified by name and their work discussed in

> **Hans-Joachim Schulze.** *Studien zur Bach-Überlieferung im 18. Jahrhundert,* **101–25. Leipzig, 1984.**

Three anonymous Weimar copyists whose work appears in parts and scores of Bach's church cantatas were assigned the sigla Anonymous Weimar 1/2/3; see

Alfred Dürr. *Studien über die frühen Kantaten Johann Sebastian Bachs.* 2d edn, 236. Wiesbaden, 1977.

Further research on Bach's early copyists is presented in

Yoshitake Kobayashi. "Quellenkundliche Überlegungen zur Chronologie der Weimarer Vokalwerke Bachs." In *Das Frühwerk Johann Sebastian Bachs: Kolloquium veranstaltet vom Institut für Musikwissenschaft der Universität Rostock 11.–13. September 1990,* edited by Karl Heller and Hans-Joachim Schulze, 290–310. Cologne, 1995.

Sigla for anonymous copyists of Bach sources were also assigned in the standard catalogue of Berlin Bach materials,

Paul Kast. *Die Bach-Handschriften der Berliner Staatsbibliothek.* Tübinger Bach-Studien 2/3. Trossingen, 1958.

Kast's sigla for J.S. Bach's copyists (*An1–*) are little used, but those for C.P.E. Bach's copyists (*An300–*) and for copyists whose work appears in the so-called Amalienbibliothek (*An400–*) do frequently appear in Bach studies. See also *5.2.4 Libraries and catalogues.*

The anonymous copyists of Bach's works in the Amalienbibliothek were also assigned sigla in

Eva Renate Wutta [Blechschmidt]. *Die Amalien-Bibliothek: Musikbibliothek der Prinzessin Anna Amalia von Preußen (1723–1787); historische Einordnung und Katalog mit Hinweisen auf die Schreiber der Handschriften.* Berlin, 1965.

Here we present a list of Bach's principal copyists, giving their sigla from Dürr's and Dadelsen's studies and references to the most important additional literature on each.

Bach Family Members

Anna Magdalena Bach

Georg von Dadelsen. *Bemerkungen zur Handschrift Johann Sebastian Bachs, seiner Familie und seines Kreises,* 27–37. Tübinger Bach-Studien 1. Trossingen, 1957.

Carl Philipp Emanuel Bach

Andreas Glöckner. "Neuerkenntnisse zu Johann Sebastian Bachs Aufführungskalender zwischen 1729 und 1735." *BJ* 67 (1981): 43–75, at 44–56.

Gottfried Heinrich Bach (=Anon. Vp?)

Georg von Dadelsen. *Bemerkungen zur Handschrift Johann Sebastian Bachs, seiner Familie und seines Kreises,* 19. Tübinger Bach-Studien 1. Trossingen, 1957.

Georg von Dadelsen. NBA V/4 KB, 89–90.

Johann Christian Bach

Hans-Joachim Schulze. "Frühe Schriftzeugnisse der beiden jüngsten Bach-Söhne." *BJ* 50 (1963/64): 61–69.

Johann Christoph Friedrich Bach (=Anon. Vq)

Hans-Joachim Schulze. "Frühe Schriftzeugnisse der beiden jüngsten Bach-Söhne." *BJ* 50 (1963/64): 61–69.

Wilhelm Friedemann Bach

Georg von Dadelsen. *Bemerkungen zur Handschrift Johann Sebastian Bachs, seiner Familie und seines Kreises,* 17–19. Tübinger Bach-Studien 1. Trossingen, 1957.

Johann Gottfried Walther

Kirsten Beißwenger. "Zur Chronologie der Notenhandschriften Johann Gottfried Walthers." In *Acht kleine Präludien und Studien über Bach: Georg von Dadelsen zum 70. Geburtstag,* **edited by Kollegium des Johann-Sebastian-Bach-Instituts Göttingen, 11–39. Wiesbaden, 1992.**

Principal Leipzig Copyists

Hauptkop. A/Anonymous 3   Johann Andreas Kuhnau

Werner Neumann. NBA I/4 KB, 16.

Hauptkop. B/Anonymous 1   Christian Gottlob Meißner

Hans-Joachim Schulze. *Studien zur Bach-Überlieferung im 18. Jahrhundert,* 101–10. Leipzig, 1984.

Hauptkop. C/Anonymous 2   Johann Heinrich Bach

Hans-Joachim Schulze. *Studien zur Bach-Überlieferung im 18. Jahrhundert,* 110–19. Leipzig, 1984.

Hauptkop. D   Samuel Gottlieb Heder

Hans-Joachim Schulze. "Johann Sebastian Bachs Konzerte—Fragen der Überlieferung und Chronologie." In *Beiträge zum Konzertschaffen Johann Sebastian Bachs*, edited by Peter Ahnsehl, Karl Heller and Hans-Joachim Schulze, 19; 25, n. 82. Bach-Studien 6. Leipzig, 1981.

Hauptkop. E   Johann Gottlob Haupt

Walter Blankenburg and Alfred Dürr. NBA II/6 KB, 124, n. 19.

Hauptkop. F=Anon. IVb   Johann Ludwig Dietel

Andreas Glöckner. "Neuerkenntnisse zu Johann Sebastian Bachs Aufführungskalender zwischen 1729 und 1735." *BJ* 67 (1981): 43–75, at 57–69.

Hauptkop. G=Anon. Vk   Rudolph Straube

Hans-Joachim Schulze. "'Das Stück in Goldpapier'—Ermittlungen zu einigen Bach-Abschriften des frühen 18. Jahrhunderts." *BJ* 64 (1978): 42, n. 91.

Hauptkop. H/Anonymous 4   [Unidentified]

Other Leipzig Students and Assistants

Johann Friedrich Agricola

Alfred Dürr. "Zur Chronologie der Handschrift Johann Christoph Altnickols und Johann Friedrich Agricolas." *BJ* 56 (1970): 44–65.

Johann Christoph Altnickol

Alfred Dürr. "Zur Chronologie der Handschrift Johann Christoph Altnickols und Johann Friedrich Agricolas." *BJ* 56 (1970): 44–65.

Christian Gottlieb Gerlach (=Anon. Ij)

Hans-Joachim Schulze. "Beiträge zur Bach-Quellenforschung." In *Bericht über den internationalen musikwissenschaftlichen Kongress Leipzig 1966*, edited by Carl Dahlhaus et al., 269–75. Cassel, 1970.

Johann Christian Köpping (=Anon. Id)

Hans-Joachim Schulze. "Beiträge zur Bach-Quellenforschung." In *Bericht über den internationalen musikwissenschaftlichen Kongress Leipzig 1966,* **edited by Carl Dahlhaus et al., 269–75. Cassel, 1970.**

Johann Ludwig Krebs

Georg von Dadelsen. *Bemerkungen zur Handschrift Johann Sebastian Bachs, seiner Familie und seines Kreises,* 23. **Tübinger Bach-Studien 1. Trossingen, 1957.**

Johann Christian Lindner (=Anon. Ik)

Friedrich Christian Samuel Mohrheim (=Anon. Vg)

Walter Blankenburg and Alfred Dürr. NBA II/6 KB, 124.

David Salomon Reichhardt (=Anon. IIIf)

Hans-Joachim Schulze. "Beiträge zur Bach-Quellenforschung." In *Bericht über den internationalen musikwissenschaftlichen Kongress Leipzig 1966,* **edited by Carl Dahlhaus et al., 269–75. Cassel, 1970.**

Paul Christian Stolle (=Anon. Vs)

Hans-Joachim Schulze. *Studien zur Bach-Überlieferung im 18. Jahrhundert,* 108–9. **Leipzig, 1984.**

5.1.4 Papers

The standard reference on the papers used in Bach's original parts, scores and documents is

Wisso Weiss and Yoshitake Kobayashi. *Katalog der Wasserzeichen in Bachs Originalhandschriften.* 2 vols. NBA ix/1. **Cassel and Leipzig, 1985.**

The text volume describes the papers used by Bach, lists the manuscripts in which each appears, and relates what is known about its origin and manufacture. There is a detailed introductory essay on papermaking, paper studies, and Bach's use of paper. The accompanying illustrative volume contains full-size tracings of the watermarks in each of the papers. (These volumes are the published version of a working document on Bach's papers prepared in 1954 for the editors of the NBA, to which references will often be found in that edition's critical commentaries.)

The studies by Dürr and Kobayashi cited in *7.2.2 Chronologies of Bach's vocal music* made particularly strong contributions to knowledge of Bach's papers.

An excellent English-language essay on paper, papermaking, and musicological paper studies is

Alan Tyson. "New dating methods: watermarks and paper-studies." In his *Mozart: studies of the autograph scores*, 1–22. Cambridge, Mass., 1987.

5.1.5 Original editions

A small group of J.S. Bach's compositions were published during his lifetime. The following studies deal with broader issues in the printed works; see also the literature on individual works and collections:

Georg Kinsky. *Die Originalausgaben der Werke Johann Sebastian Bachs.* Vienna, 1937.

Gregory G. Butler. "Leipziger Stecher in Bachs Originaldrucken." *BJ* 66 (1980): 9–26.

Gregory Butler. *Bach's Clavier-Übung III: the making of a print; with a companion study of the Canonic Variations on "Vom Himmel Hoch," BWV 769.* Durham, 1990.

Christoph Wolff. "Ordnungsprinzipien in den Originaldrucken Bachscher Werke." In *Bach-Interpretationen,* edited by Martin Geck, 144–67. Göttingen, 1969. Translated by Alfred Mann as "Principles of design and order in Bach's original editions." In Wolff, *Bach: essays on his life and music,* 340–58. Cambridge, Mass., 1991.

5.2 Transmission

A large part of the collective effort of Bach research in the late twentieth century has concerned itself with transmission (Überlieferung): how Bach's music and its sources circulated and were passed along from year to year. Largely because so little of Bach's music was published under his supervision, we depend on the survival of fragile autographs and student and family copies for our knowledge of what Bach composed and for the musical texts of his works. Conflicting texts in different copies, misattributions, and the loss both of primary and secondary sources—not least in World War II—have shown how important it is to ask when, where, and with whom a source of Bach's music originated. In addition, there has been growing interest in the circulation of Bach's music in his own lifetime. These questions have fostered an enormous literature on the transmission of Bach's music among family members, students, collectors, and libraries.

The most important work on the early transmission of Bach's music, largely containing updated versions of studies published elsewhere, is

Hans-Joachim Schulze. *Studien zur Bach-Überlieferung im 18. Jahrhundert.* Leipzig, 1984.

5.2.1 Bach's estate and its division

When J.S. Bach died, his estate was divided among family members. Two legal documents survive: the valuation of his estate (*Dok* II/627; *BR,* 191–97) and the division of the estate (*Dok* II/628). These documents are concerned primarily with money, furniture, household articles, musical instruments, and books, which are enumerated. On the books, see *4.2 Bach's library.*

Bach's musical materials are not mentioned in these documents. The division of Bach's music library (both his own music and that of other composers) has been the subject of much research. On the materials owned by the various heirs (principally Anna Magdalena, Wilhelm Friedemann, Carl Philipp Emanuel, Johann Christian, and Johann Christoph Friedrich Bach), see *5.2.2 Bach's heirs.* For an overview of the division of the estate, see

Yoshitake Kobayashi. "Zur Teilung des Bachschen Erbes." In *Acht kleine Präludien und Studien über Bach: Georg von Dadelsen zum 70. Geburtstag,* edited by Kollegium des Johann-Sebastian-Bach-Instituts Göttingen, 67–75. Wiesbaden, 1992.

Kirsten Beißwenger. *Johann Sebastian Bachs Notenbibliothek,* 102–12. Cassel, 1992.

The greatest attention has been given to the division of the church cantatas; see

Alfred Dürr, Robert Freeman and James Webster. NBA I/15 KB, 205ff.

Alfred Dürr. *Zur Chronologie der Leipziger Vokalwerke J.S. Bachs.* 2d ed., 11–20. Cassel, 1976.

On the much-debated question of the number of church cantata cycles and the inheritance of their sources, see *7.3.1 Cantatas*.

5.2.2 Bach's heirs

There are three catalogues of material from the estate of C.P.E. Bach, who is the best-documented heir of J.S. Bach. They include music by J.S. Bach as well as books and music by other composers that definitely or possibly belonged to J.S. Bach.

Books and music sold shortly after Emanuel's death are listed in
Verzeichniß auserlesener . . . Bücher . . . nebst einigen Musikalien und Kupferstichen welche am 11 August und folgende Tage . . . öffentlich verkauft werden sollen. Hamburg, 1789. Exemplar Brussels, Koninklijke Bibliotheek Albert I., Afdeling Muziek, Fonds Fétis 5177 A8.

For a facsimile and commentary, see
Ulrich Leisinger. "Die 'Bachsche Auction' von 1789." *BJ* 77 (1991): 97–126.

The principal catalogue of Emanuel's musical estate, in a form he probably prepared himself, is
Verzeichniß des musikalischen Nachlasses des verstorbenen Capellmeisters Carl Philipp Emanuel Bach. Hamburg, 1790.

Facsimile edition:
The catalog of Carl Philipp Emanuel Bach's estate, edited by Rachel W. Wade. New York, 1981.

Transcriptions may be found in
Heinrich Miesner. "Philipp Emanuel Bachs musikalischer Nachlass." *BJ* 35 (1938): 103–36; 36 (1939): 81–112; 37 (1940–48): 161–81. [complete]

Dok III/957 [portions relating directly to J.S. Bach]

A catalogue of the sale of leftovers from Emanuel's estate:
Verzeichniß von auserlesenen . . . meistens Neuen Büchern und Kostbaren Werken . . . welche nebst den Musikalien aus dem Nachlaß des seel.

Kapellmeisters C.P.E. Bach . . . öffentlicht verkauft werden sollen. Hamburg, [1805]. Exemplar SBB Mus. Db 313.

Note that until the discovery of the first catalogue listed above, this third catalogue was thought to represent the "Bachische Auction" mentioned in connection with numerous Bach sources. There is a transcription of the relevant portions in the notes to *Dok* III/957.

There are no documents for other heirs of J.S. Bach comparable to the catalogues of C.P.E. Bach's estate. On Wilhelm Friedemann's materials from his father, see

Peter Wollny. "Studies in the music of Wilhelm Friedemann Bach: sources and style." Ph.D. diss. Harvard University, 1993.

The largest body of material known to have been inherited by Anna Magdalena Bach consists of the original performing parts for Bach's second Leipzig cantata cycle, which passed to the St. Thomas School. See

Werner Neumann and Christine Fröde. *Die Bach-Handschriften der Thomasschule Leipzig: Katalog.* Beiträge zur Bachforschung 5. Leipzig, 1986.

5.2.3 Collectors and collections

Many Bach sources were preserved by private collectors. The most important are listed here, with literature on their collections.

Bernhard Christoph Breitkopf (1695–1777) and Johann Gottlob Immanuel Breitkopf (1719–1794)

The publishing house of Bernhard Christoph Breitkopf (1695–1777) and his son Johann Gottlob Immanuel Breitkopf (1719–1794) was important in early Bach transmission. Their catalogues offered printed and manuscript music by and associated with Bach, and they owned many original sources of Bach's music.

Bach-related excerpts from their catalogues are reproduced in *Dok* III/705, 711, and 718. An overview of their trade in Bach manuscripts is

Yoshitake Kobayashi. "Breitkopfs Handel mit Bach-Handschriften." Beiträge zur Bachforschung 1 (1982): 79–84.

Their role in the transmission of organ works is examined in

Ernest May. "Breitkopf's role in the transmission of J.S. Bach's organ chorales." Ph.D. diss. Princeton University, 1974.

Recent essays on several aspects of Bach and the Breitkopfs are published in
> George Stauffer, ed. *J.S. Bach, the Breitkopfs, and eighteenth-century music trade.* Bach perspectives 2. Lincoln, 1996.

Johann Nikolaus Mempell (1713–1747) and Johann Gottlieb Preller (1727–1786)

The so-called Mempell-Preller collection, which contains important sources for Bach's keyboard music, was compiled by the cantors Mempell and Preller. Much of the collection is now in the Musikbibliothek der Stadt Leipzig. See the catalogue of that collection in *5.2.4 Libraries and catalogues* and
> Hans-Joachim Schulze. *Studien zur Bach-Überlieferung im 18. Jahrhundert*, 69–88. Leipzig, 1984.

Princess Anna Amalia of Prussia (1723–1787)

Anna Amalia, the sister of King Frederick the Great of Prussia, studied music under Bach's student J.P. Kirnberger. For a catalogue of her library, see
> Eva Renate Blechschmidt [Wutta]. *Die Amalien-Bibliothek: Musikbibliothek der Prinzessin Anna Amalia von Preußen (1723–1787; historische Einordnung und Katalog mit Hinweisen auf die Schreiber der Handschriften.* Berlin, 1965.

> Eva Renate Wutta. *Quellen der Bach-Tradition in der Berliner Amalien-Bibliothek mit zahlreichen Abbildungen von Handschriften nebst Briefen der Anna Amalia von Preußen (1723–1787).* Tutzing, 1989.

Otto Karl Friedrich von Voß (1755–1823) and descendants [Voß-Buch]

In 1851 the Royal Library in Berlin acquired the collection belonging to the Berlin Voß family. The music is catalogued in
> *Verzeichnis von den Musicalien des Konigl: Würkl. Geheimen Etats-Kriegs- und dirigierenden Ministre, pp Herrn Freiherrn von Voß, Excellenz.* SBB Mus. ms. theor. Kat. 21.

Concerning the Bach materials, see
> Bettina Faulstich. "Die Werke Johann Sebastian Bachs in der Musikaliensammlung der Familie von Voss." In *Jahrbuch des Staatlichen Instituts für Musikforschung Preußischer Kulturbesitz, 1993*, 131–40. Stuttgart, 1993.

Carl Friedrich Zelter (1758–1832) / Berlin Sing-Akademie

Zelter was the longtime director of the Sing-Akademie zu Berlin and an early proponent of Bach's music, especially the sacred vocal works, which he rehearsed and performed. The Sing-Akademie's music collection, which eventually included Zelter's estate and items from the collection of Georg Poelchau (its librarian), contained much Bach material, including many original sources. The Sing-Akademie sold most of its Bach manuscripts to the Royal Library in Berlin in 1854; the remainder of its collection vanished during World War II.

On the Sing-Akademie in general, see
Georg Schünemann. *Die Singakademie zu Berlin 1791–1941.* Regensburg, 1941.

On its Bach activities, see
Georg Schünemann. "Die Bachpflege der Berliner Singakademie." *BJ* 25 (1928): 138–71.

For a recollection of its music collection, lost since the 1940s, see
Friedrich Welter. "Die Musikbibliothek der Sing-Akademie zu Berlin: Versuch eines Nachweises ihrer früheren Bestände." In *Sing-Akademie zu Berlin: Festschrift zu 175jährigen Bestehen,* edited by Werner Bollert, 33–47. Berlin, 1966.

On its Bach holdings, see
Werner Neumann. "Welche Handschriften J.S. Bachscher Werke besaß die Berliner Singakademie?" In *Hans Albrecht in Memoriam,* edited by Wilfried Brennecke and Hans Haase, 136–42. Cassel, 1962.

Catalogues of Zelter's estate:
***Catalog musikalisch- literarischer und practischer Werke aus dem Nachlasse der Königl: Professors Dr. Zelter.* Manuscript. SBB N. Mus ms. theor. 30.**

***Carl Friedrich Zelter: Verzeichnis seiner musikalischen Bibliothek.* Manuscript. Tokyo, Nanki Music Library M 01/80 Ms.**

Hans Georg Nägeli (1773–1836)

Nägeli was a composer, publisher, and performer, principally in Zurich. On his Bach collection see
Detlef Gojowy. "Wie entstand Hans Georg Nägelis Bach-Sammlung?

Dokumente zur Bach-Renaissance im 19. Jahrhundert." *BJ* 56 (1970): 66–104.

Raymond Meylan. "Neues zum Musikaliennachlaß von Hans Georg Nägeli." *BJ* 82 (1996): 23–47.

Georg Poelchau (1773–1836)

Poelchau was the most important collector of his time of music by Bach and every other composer. He purchased a great deal of material from the estate of C.P.E. Bach, and was a close colleague of Carl Friedrich Zelter at the Berlin Sing-Akademie. Poelchau's collection, acquired by the Royal Library in Berlin in 1841, formed the basis of its Music Division.(see *5.2.4 Libraries and catalogues*).

Poelchau's four-volume catalogue of his collection is in the Staatsbibliothek zu Berlin/Stiftung Preußischer Kulturbesitz, Musikabteilung:
  I.   Mus. ms. theor. Kat 61 [theory, history, literature]
  II. Mus. ms. theor. Kat 56 [printed music, 16th and 17th centuries]
  III. Mus. ms. theor. Kat 51 [printed music, 18th and 19th centuries]
  IV. Mus. ms. theor. Kat 41 [manuscript music]

On Poelchau and his collection, see
  Klaus Engler. "Georg Poelchau und seine Musikaliensammlung: ein Beitrag zur Überlieferung Bachscher Musik in der ersten Hälfte des 19. Jahrhunderts." Ph.D. diss. University of Tübingen, 1984.

Franz Hauser (1794–1870)

Hauser, a singer and teacher, compiled a large collection of Bach's music. The three catalogues of his collection, much of which was acquired by the State Library in Berlin in 1904, are transcribed and annotated in
  Yoshitake Kobayashi. "Franz Hauser und seine Bach-Handschriften-sammlung." Ph.D. diss. University of Göttingen, 1973.

This work also contains detailed information on other Bach collectors whose materials Hauser acquired, including Johann Gottfried Schicht, Johann Gottlob Schuster, and the Mempell-Preller collection.

Aloys Fuchs (1799–1853)

Collector in Vienna. See
  Friedrich Wilhelm Riedel. "Aloys Fuchs als Sammler Bachscher Werke." *BJ* 47 (1960): 83–99.

Philipp Spitta (1841–1894)

Much (but not all) of the collection of the Bach biographer Philipp Spitta recently resurfaced in Poland. See

Christoph Wolff. "From Berlin to Lódz: the Spitta Collection resurfaces." *Notes* **46 (1989): 311–27.**

Manfred Gorke (1897–1956)

The collection of Gorke, a banker, was acquired in 1935 by the Musikbibliothek der Stadt Leipzig. See

Hans-Joachim Schulze. *Katalog der Sammlung Manfred Gorke: Bachiana und andere Handschriften und Drucke des 18. und frühen 19. Jahrhunderts.* **Leipzig, 1977.**

5.2.4 Libraries and catalogues

Bach sources are found in libraries throughout the world. Here we discuss a few of the most important collections for Bach research.

The Berlin Libraries

The most important library for Bach studies is the Music Division of the main library in Berlin, known by several different names in its tumultuous history. It is necessary to understand this history to interpret the changing references to the library and its holdings.

At the time the Musikabteilung (music division) was founded in 1824, the library was known as the Königliche Bibliothek (Royal Library); it was later renamed the Preußische Staatsbibliothek (Prussian State Library). During World War II, its holdings were dispersed, and, when recovered, were split between two institutions, one in East Berlin and one in West Berlin. Items recovered from Eastern sectors were returned to East Berlin in the German Democratic Republic, in quarters near the prewar site on Unter den Linden; this library was known as the Deutsche Staatsbibliothek (DSB). (Some items from Eastern sectors ended up in Craców; see below in this section.) Items recovered from Western sectors were housed temporarily in the university towns of Tübingen and Marburg in an entity known as the Westdeutsche Bibliothek, then moved to the new quarters of the Staatsbibliothek Preußischer Kulturbesitz (SPK) in West Berlin.

With the reunification of Germany in 1990, the two institutions were merged into the Staatsbibliothek zu Berlin/Stiftung Preußischer Kulturbesitz (SBB). The music Division was at first split between the two buildings, but in 1997 was consolidated on Unter den Linden.

On the history of the collection see
Karl-Heinz Köhler. "Die Bach-Sammlung der Deutschen Staatsbibliothek—Überlieferung und Bedeutung." Bach-Studien 5 (1975): 139–46.

The unparalleled Bach holdings of the SBB include the collections of Georg Poelchau, the Voß-Buch family, Franz Hauser, and Princess Anna Amalia of Prussia. The acquisition of the library's Bach holdings is discussed in

Martin Tielke. "Die Erwerbung der Bach-Autographen durch die Königliche Bibliothek / Preußische Staatsbibliothek in Berlin." Thesis, Bibliothekar-Lehrinstitut des Landes Nordrhein-Westfalen, Cologne, 1980.

This study also traces the provenance of Bach autographs not traced in Kast's catalogue, and includes an extremely useful list of library and collectors' catalogues, estate catalogues, and acquisition lists of collections that are now part of the SBB Music Division.

The card catalogue of the Music Division is available on microfiche:
Deutsche Staatsbibliothek. Musikabteilung. *Alphabetischer Katalog der Musikabteilung der Deutschen Staatsbibliothek zu Berlin.* Hildesheim, 1990.

The basic catalogue of its Bach manuscripts, in need of updating but still indispensable, is
Paul Kast. *Die Bach-Handschriften der Berliner Staatsbibliothek.* Tübinger Bach-Studien 2/3. Trossingen, 1958.

This volume identifies the provenance, contents, and copyists of the Bach holdings, most of which carry shelf numbers beginning with "Mus. ms. autogr. Bach P" (Partitur=score) or "Mus. ms. autogr. Bach St" (Stimmen=parts). In the Bach literature, these are usually abbreviated to just P and St; for example, the autograph score of the *St. Matthew Passion* is known as SBB P 25, or just P 25. Manuscript music of other composers has shelf numbers beginning with "Mus. ms." (A new catalogue of the SBB's Bach materials is in preparation by Joachim Jaenecke.)
Address: Staatsbibliothek zu Berlin—Preußischer Kulturbesitz, Musikabteilung mit Mendelssohn-Archiv, Unter den Linden 8, D-10117 Berlin, Germany.

On the (lost) collection of the Sing-Akademie zu Berlin, see *5.2.3 Collectors and collections.*

Biblioteka Jagiellonska, Craców, Poland

The Jagellonian University Library is important to Bach studies because a number of original Bach sources (along with autographs of Mozart and Beethoven and many important music prints) from the State Library in Berlin ended up there in the wake of World War II (see above on the history of the Berlin libraries).

The survival of the material from Berlin was a closely guarded secret. Its rediscovery in the late 1970s is grippingly told in

Nigel Lewis. *Paperchase: Mozart, Beethoven, Bach . . . the search for their lost music.* London, 1981.

There is no formal catalogue of the Bach materials now in Craców; they constitute most of the scores and parts listed in Kast's catalogue as missing. The items are still catalogued under their old Berlin call numbers.

Address: Biblioteka Jagiellonska, Aleja Mickiewicza 22, Craców, Poland.

Leipzig libraries

Leipzig Bach materials are divided among several libraries. The holdings of the St. Thomas School library, principally the original performing parts for Bach's second cantata cycle, are part of the collection of the Bach-Archiv, Leipzig. The materials are catalogued in

Werner Neumann and Christine Fröde. *Die Bach-Handschriften der Thomasschule Leipzig: Katalog.* Beiträge zur Bachforschung 5. Leipzig, 1986.

Address: Bach-Archiv, Postfach 101349, 04023 Leipzig, Germany.

The Musikbibliothek der Stadt Leipzig holds a great deal of Bach material, including the Gorke Collection and most of the Mempell-Preller Collection. On its Bach holdings, see

Peter Krause. *Handschriften der Werke Johann Sebastian Bachs in der Musikbibliothek der Stadt Leipzig.* Leipzig, 1964.

Peter Krause. *Originalausgaben und ältere Drucke der Werke Johann Sebastian Bachs in der Musikbibliothek der Stadt Leipzig.* Leipzig, 1970.

Address: Musikbibliothek der Stadt Leipzig, Wilhelm-Leuschner-Platz 10/11, 04107 Leipzig, Germany.

Austrian National Library, Vienna

The Austrian National Library is important to Bach studies because of Anthony von Hoboken's comprehensive collection of early printed editions of Bach's music. A catalogue of the collection is available:

Institut für österreichische Musikdokumentation. *Katalog der Sammlung Anthony van Hoboken in der Musiksammlung der Österreichischen Nationalbibliothek: musikalische Erst- und Frühdrucke.* Vol. 1. *Johann Sebastian Bach und seine Söhne.* **Edited by Thomas Leibnitz. Tutzing, 1982.**

The J.S. Bach prints themselves are available on microfiche:

Österreichische Nationalbibliothek: Musiksammlung. *Die Sammlung Hoboken in der Musiksammlung der Österreichischen Nationalbibliothek, Teil 1—Johann Sebastian Bach: die Bach-Drucke.* **Hildesheim, 1982.**

Address: Österreichische Nationalbibliothek, Musiksammlung, Augustinerstraße 1, A-1014 Vienna, Austria.

American libraries and collections

The following volume discusses in detail the Bach sources of various kinds located in the United States at the time of its compilation.

Gerhard Herz. *Bach-Quellen in Amerika / Bach sources in America.* **Cassel, 1984.**

6

Repertory and editions

6.1 Worklists

Many Bach biographies include complete or nearly complete lists of his works, typically by genre. The most valuable are those that also point the reader to editions. By far the best worklist is that by Richard Jones in

Christoph Wolff and Walter Emery. "Bach, Johann Sebastian." In *The New Grove dictionary of music and musicians,* **edited by Stanley Sadie, vol. 1, 818–36. London, 1980. Rev. in Christoph Wolff et al.** *The New Grove Bach family,* **178–214. New York, 1983. Further rev. in translation as** *Die Bach-Familie,* **193–254. Stuttgart, 1993.**

This list provides the works' BWV numbers, titles, remarks on scoring and dating, and volume and page references in the BG and NBA (the complete-works editions discussed below). Notice that there are some changes to the worklist in the 1983 and 1993 versions.

To locate vocal compositions and individual movements by their texts, see the resources listed in *7.1.1 Texts.*

To locate Bach works by their musical themes, consult
May deForest McAll. *Melodic index to the works of Johann Sebastian Bach.* **Rev. ed. New York, 1962, and reprints.**

McAll provides finding charts of basic melodic patterns and then tabulates Bach themes according to those three-interval patterns (excluding repeated notes and ornaments). She also provides the works' titles, BWV numbers, and locations in the BG.

6.2 Editions

6.2.1 Early editions

A list of Bach editions preceding the publication of his complete works in the BG is found in

Max Schneider. "Verzeichnis der bis zum Jahre 1851 gedruckten (und der geschrieben im Handel gewesenen) Werke von Johann Sebastian Bach." *BJ* [3] (1906): 84–113.

The Austrian National Library houses Anthony von Hoboken's comprehensive collection of early printed editions of Bach's music. A catalogue of the collection is available:

Institut für österreichische Musikdokumentation. *Katalog der Sammlung Anthony van Hoboken in der Musiksammlung der Österreichischen Nationalbibliothek: musikalische Erst- und Frühdrucke.* Vol. 1. *Johann Sebastian Bach und seine Söhne.* **Edited by Thomas Leibnitz. Tutzing, 1982.**

The J.S. Bach prints themselves are available on microfiche:

Österreichische Nationalbibliothek: Musiksammlung. *Die Sammlung Hoboken in der Musiksammlung der Österreichischen Nationalbibliothek, Teil 1—Johann Sebastian Bach: die Bach-Drucke.* **Hildesheim, 1982.**

For an example of a detailed study of early editions, see
Magali Philippsborn. "Die Frühdrucke der Werke Johann Sebastian Bachs in der ersten Hälfte des 19. Jahrhunderts: eine kritisch vergleichende Untersuchung anhand des Wohltemperierten Klaviers I." Ph.D. diss. University of Frankfurt am Main, 1975.

See also *5.1.5 Original editions.*

6.2.2 Bach-Gesellschaft edition

The BG (Bach-Gesellschaft) edition was published by Breitkopf and Härtel in the second half of the nineteenth century. It was printed in Jahrgänge (annual installments), but their actual publication, as shown by the preface dates, did not always conform to this production schedule.

The principal concern was to provide users with all of Bach's music in clean and easy-to-read printed scores, free of later additions. The prefaces, except in the cases of some larger and more well-known works (for example, the *St. Matthew Passion*), are typically short and almost perfunctory. They feature limited information about the sources: usually only their location, their wrapper's or heading's wording, and a list of their few uncorrected copying errors. The later volumes also provide illustrations of watermarks. When appropriate, some volumes comment generally and briefly on how they differ from previous editions. The editors do not distinguish Bach's copyists, give detailed information on provenance, nor do they evaluate the early sources of a work.

There are several useful indexes within the BG itself. Vol. 27.2 is a list of incipits for the cantatas BWV 1–120. Vol. 46 features a host of indexes: Incipits for cantatas 121–91, related compositions, and the remaining vocal works, pp. 3–164; Church cantatas by liturgical assignment, pp. 165–67; Arias by voice type, pp. 167–71; Vocal duets and trios, pp. 171–72; Arias by their solo instrument, instrumental movements, pp. 172–76; Index of first lines, pp. 176–90; Incipits of instrumental works, pp. 191–245; Overview of the instrumental works (alphabetical by title and by movement type), pp. 246–52; Persons and places mentioned in the prefaces, pp. 253–62; Bach's works, by BG vol., p. 263; Bach's works, by genre, pp. 263–66; List of indexes, p. 266.

Many current Bach study scores (for example, Dover, Kalmus, Lea Pocket Scores) are reproductions of BG editions.

Here we list basic information about the volumes of the BG.

Johann Sebastian Bachs Werke. Edited by the Bach-Gesellschaft of Leipzig, Leipzig, 1851–99.

Vol.	Contents	Editor	Date
1	Church cantatas: BWV 1–10	M. Hauptmann	1851
2	Church cantatas: BWV 11–20	M. Hauptmann	1852
3	Inventions and Sinfonias, *Clavier-Übung* I–IV, BWV 910–11, 944	C.F. Becker	1853
4	*St. Matthew Passion:* BWV 244	Julius Rietz, Wilhelm Rust [rev. ed. by Max Seiffert, 1935]	1854
5.1	Church cantatas and secular cantata: BWV 21–30, 30a (movements 2, 4, 6, 8, 10–12, libretto)	Wilhelm Rust	1855
5.2	*Christmas Oratorio:* BWV 248	Wilhelm Rust	1856
6	*Mass in B minor:* BWV 232	Julius Rietz	1856, rev. ed. 1857
7	Church cantatas: BWV 31–40	Wilhelm Rust	1857
8	Masses: BWV 233–36	M. Hauptmann	1858
9	Chamber music: BWV 1030–32, 1025, 1014–19, 1027–29, 1038, 1037, 1039, 1020	Wilhelm Rust	1860
10	Church cantatas: BWV 41–50	Wilhelm Rust	1860
11.1	*Magnificat:* BWV 243, 243a (four Christmas interpolations); Mass movements: 237–40	Wilhelm Rust	1862
11.2	Secular cantatas: BWV 201–205	Wilhelm Rust	1862

12.1	*St. John Passion*: BWV 245	Wilhelm Rust	1863
12.2	Church cantatas: BWV 51–60	Wilhelm Rust	1863
13.1	Wedding cantatas: BWV 195–97; wedding chorales: BWV 250–52	Wilhelm Rust	1864
13.2	*English Suites, French Suites* [cf. vol. 45.1]	[Franz Espagne—see *Die Musikforschung* 6 (1953): 356–57]	1865
13.3	*Trauerode*: BWV 198	Wilhelm Rust	1865
14	*Well-Tempered Clavier* I–II, variants	Franz Kroll	1866
15	Organ works: BWV 525–30, 531–48, 564–66, 582	Wilhelm Rust	1867
16	Church cantatas: BWV 61–70, 69a	Wilhelm Rust	1868
17	Harpsichord concertos: BWV 1052–59; Triple Concerto: BWV 1044	Wilhelm Rust	1869
18	Church cantatas: BWV 71–80	Wilhelm Rust	1870
19	*Brandenburg Concertos*: BWV 1046–51	Wilhelm Rust	1871
20.1	Church cantatas: BWV 81–90	Wilhelm Rust	1872
20.2	Secular cantatas: BWV 206, 207, 207a (movements 2, 4, 6)	Wilhelm Rust	1873
21.1	Violin concertos: BWV 1041–43, 1045	Wilhelm Rust	1874
21.2	Concertos for two harpsichords: BWV 1060–62	Wilhelm Rust	1874
21.3	*Easter Oratorio*: BWV 249	Wilhelm Rust	1874
22	Church cantatas: BWV 91–100	Wilhelm Rust	1875

(cont'd)

Johann Sebastian Bachs Werke, Bach-Gesellschaft, *continued*

Vol.	Contents	Editor	Date
23	Church cantatas: BWV 101–10	Wilhelm Rust	1876
24	Church cantatas: BWV 111–20	Alfred Dörffel	1876
25.1	*Art of Fugue* (original ed.), *Art of Fugue* (ms.): BWV 1080	Wilhelm Rust	1878
25.2	Organ works: *Orgelbüchlein*, Schübler chorales, Leipzig chorales, variants	Wilhelm Rust	1878
26	Church cantatas: BWV 121–30	Alfred Dörffel	1878
27.1	Solo violin and cello works: BWV 1001–12	Alfred Dörffel	1879
27.2	Thematic index to church cantatas BWV 1–120	Alfred Dörffel	1878
28	Church cantatas and secular cantata: BWV 131–40, 134a (source description)	Wilhelm Rust	1881
29	Secular cantatas: BWV 208–10, 194, 211–12, 134a (fragmentarily), 210a, 1040	Paul Graf Waldersee	1881
30	Church cantatas: BWV 141–50	Paul Graf Waldersee	1884
31.1	Orchestral suites and sinfonia: BWV 1066–69, 1046a	Alfred Dörffel	1885
31.2	*Musical Offering:* BWV 1079	Alfred Dörffel	1885
31.3	Concertos for three harpsichords: BWV 1063–64	Paul Graf Waldersee	1885
32	Church cantatas: BWV 151–60	Ernst Naumann	1886
33	Church cantatas: BWV 161–70	Franz Wüllner	1887
34	Secular cantatas: BWV 173a, 36c, 36b, 213–15, 30a (only voices and bc), 207a (only voices and bc)	Paul Graf Waldersee	1887

35	Church cantatas: BWV 171–80	Alfred Dörffel	1888
36	Keyboard works: suites, toccatas, preludes, fugues, fantasias, and other pieces, variants, suite fragments, individual movements, incomplete pieces	Ernst Naumann	1890
37	Church cantatas: BWV 181–90	Alfred Dörffel	1891
38	Organ works: preludes, fugues, fantasias, and other pieces, concerto arrangements, variants, incomplete pieces, pieces of uncertain authorship, Vivaldi original movement	Ernst Naumann	1891
39	Motets: BWV 225–30, 226a, Anh. III 159, 231; chorales in the C.P.E. Bach collection, lieder and arias from the Schemelli Gesangbuch and the 1725 music book for Anna Magdalena Bach	F. Wüllner	1892
40	Organ works: "Kirnberger chorales," various chorale preludes, chorale variations, variants, incomplete pieces, pieces of uncertain authorship or corrupt transmission	Ernst Naumann	1893
41	Church cantatas: BWV 191–93, 197a; wedding cantatas: 34a, 120a; individual Mass movements: BWV 233a, 241–42; church cantatas of uncertain authorship: BWV 217–20; list of church compositions by Johann Ludwig Bach	Alfred Dörffel	1894
42	Keyboard works: arrangements, various preludes, fugues, and other pieces probably by Bach, pieces of uncertain authorship, variants, concerto 2 of Vivaldi and fugue of Erselius in their originals	Ernst Naumann	1894
43.1	Chamber works: BWV 1033–35, 1023, 1026, Anh. III 188; concerto for four harpsichords: BWV 1065; Vivaldi concerto in B minor for four violins in its original	Paul Graf Waldersee	1894
43.2	Pieces from the music books for Anna Magdalena Bach	Paul Graf Waldersee	1894

(cont'd)

Johann Sebastian Bachs Werke, Bach-Gesellschaft, *continued*

Vol.	Contents	Editor	Date
44	Facsimile pages	H. Kretzschmar	1895
45.1	[Rev. ed. of vol. 13.2] *English Suites, French Suites*	Ernst Naumann	1895
45.1[bis]	Instrumental works: canons, various compositions, keyboard book for Wilhelm Friedemann Bach, concerning BWV 1041, concerning BWV 188, concerning the *Well-Tempered Clavier* I–II	Alfred Dörffel	1897
45.2	Anon.: *St. Luke Passion* (formerly BWV 246)	Alfred Dörffel	1898
46	Report, thematic catalogues, indexes	H.K. Kretzschmar	1899

6.2.3 Neue Bach-Ausgabe

Following all of the activity associated with the bicentenary of Bach's death, the Johann-Sebastian-Bach-Institut Göttingen and the Bach-Archiv Leipzig launched a new complete works edition, the Neue Bach-Ausgabe. Before the reunification of Germany, the volumes were published in Cassel by Bärenreiter-Verlag and in Leipzig by the VEB [*Volkseigener Betrieb*] Deutscher Verlag für Musik. Now they are published in Cassel by Bärenreiter-Verlag.

The NBA's contents are not identical to the BG's, as some new Bach pieces have been discovered in the meantime and others determined not to be by Bach.

There are many differences between the two editions. Modern clefs are almost always used, making Bach's vocal scores easier to read for today's users. Most important, the NBA provides much more detailed descriptions, histories, and evaluations of the sources. The NBA (unlike the BG) is based on the text-critical methods employed by Karl Lachmann in his edition (1831) of the New Testament: restoring a text from multiple sources by constructing a stemma (a sort of genealogical tree, arrived at by collating the various sources' errors).

For a historical and conceptual survey of the ideas and practices involved in preparing scholarly editions like the Neue Bach-Ausgabe, see

Philip Brett. "Text, context, and the early music editor." In *Authenticity and early music: a symposium*, edited by Nicholas Kenyon, 83–114. Oxford, 1988.

The 1966 version of the editorial practices to be followed for NBA volumes was published as

"Johann Sebastian Bach: Neue Ausgabe sämtlicher Werke . . . Richtlinien für die Mitarbeiter (Fassung vom Januar 1966)." In *Editionsrichtlinien musikalischer Denkmäler und Gesamtausgaben: im Auftrag der Gesellschaft für Musikforschung*, edited by Georg von Dadelsen, 61–80. Cassel, 1967.

On the problems in deciding which works are really by Bach and thus should be printed in the NBA, see

Klaus Hofmann. "Bach oder nicht Bach? Die Neue Bach-Ausgabe und das Echtheitsproblem: mit einem Beitrag von Yoshitake Kobayashi über 'Diplomatische Mittel der Echtheitskritik.'" In *Opera Incerta: Echtheitsfragen als Problem musikwissenschaftlicher Gesamtausgaben—Kolloquium Mainz 1988*, edited by Hans-Peter Bennwitz et al., 9–69. Stuttgart, 1991.

Use of the NBA music volumes is relatively straightforward. All headings, tempo markings, scorings, trills, and so on indicated in italics are editorial. Each volume of the NBA is meant to be used in conjunction with its accompanying critical report (Kritischer Bericht), which lists various sorts of information in four sections.

1. *Die Quellen* (the sources). The standard procedure is first to describe the autograph score and original parts (if they survive). General information about provenance is followed by extremely detailed lists of the page-by-page contents of the manuscripts and identification of the scribes. All corrections and revisions of earlier readings are duly noted. Then follow shorter descriptions of other early manuscripts, information about early printings, lists of lost sources, and comparison material (for example, printed versions of librettos).

Some of the most involved work for the editor to produce—and for the user to read—is the subsection *Zur Abhängigkeit der Quellen* (on the sources' relationship to each other). Although for some works this subsection turns out to be straightforward and short, for others it can get long and quite complicated (see, for example, the critical reports for the organ works in ser. IV, vols. 5–6, or the *St. John Passion*). This subsection's significance is of course most crucial in the instances where Bach's own materials do not survive.

2. *Allgemeines* (general matters). Here the editor discusses various issues concerning the librettist, the dating of the original and subsequent performances under Bach's direction, the pitch standards, the scoring (for example, determining the meaning of ambiguous indications such as "corno"), and the texts to be assigned to chorale movements in vocal works when Bach's original parts or sources copied from them do not survive.

3. *Ausgaben* (editions). Here the editor notes previous scholarly editions of the work (in many cases the BG is all there was) and their merits and problems.

4. *Spezielle Anmerkungen* (particular observations). Here the editor meticulously notes the differences among the sources that were employed to produce the NBA's music volume; that is, on the basis of the conclusions from the section *Zur Abhängigkeit der Quellen*, certain sources may not be used at all to produce the NBA's readings.

A useful guide to the NBA's music volumes and critical reports, showing their relevance to performance, appeared as

Alfred Dürr. "Wissenschaftliche Neuausgaben und die Praxis: eine Gebrauchsanleitung zum Lesen Kritischer Berichte, dargestellt an der Neuen Bach-Ausgabe." *Musik und Kirche* **29 (1959): 77–82.**

Here we list basic information about the NBA, by volume. (The publication dates can prove useful in determining which volumes postdate the BWV and BC.)

The four volumes of *Bach-Dokumente* are supplements to the NBA. See *3.2.1 Documents* and *3.2.2 Iconography.*

Johann Sebastian Bach. *Neue Ausgabe sämtlicher Werke* [Neue Bach-Ausgabe]. Edited by the Johann-Sebastian-Bach-Institut Göttingen and the Bach-Archiv Leipzig. Cassel and Leipzig, 1954– .

Ser. & Vol.	*Contents* (items in parentheses only in the critical reports)	*Editor*	*Dates* (music vol./critical report)
I/1	Cantatas for Advent: BWV 61, 36, 62, 132, (70a, 186a, 147a)	Alfred Dürr, Werner Neumann	1954/55
I/2	Cantatas for Christmas Day: BWV 63, 197a, 110, 91, 191	Alfred Dürr	1957/57
I/3	Cantatas for the 2d and 3d Days of Christmas, 1st Sunday after Christmas		
I/4	Cantatas for New Year's and the Sunday after New Year's: BWV 190, 41, 16, 171, 143, 153, 58, (*Ihr wallenden Wolken*)	Werner Neumann	1965/64
I/5	Cantatas for Epiphany to the 2d Sunday after Epiphany: BWV 65, 123, 154, 124, 32, 155, 3, 13	Marianne Helms	1975/76
I/6	Cantatas for the 3d and 4th Sundays after Epiphany: BWV 73, 111, 72, 156, 81, 14	Ulrich Leisinger, Peter Wollny	1996/96
I/7	Cantatas for the 3d and 2d Sundays before Lent: BWV 144, 84, 92, 18, 181, 126	Werner Neumann	1956/57
I/8.1	Cantatas for the Sunday before Lent: BWV 22, 23, 127, 159	Christoph Wolff	1992/
I/8.2	Cantatas for Sundays in Lent (Oculi, Palm Sunday)		
I/9	Cantatas for Easter Sunday: BWV 4, 31	Alfred Dürr	1985/86

I/10	Cantatas for Easter Monday and Tuesday: BWV 66, 6, 134, 145, 158	Alfred Dürr	1955/56
I/11.1	Cantatas for the 1st and 2d Sundays after Easter: BWV 67, 42, 104, 85, 112	Reinmar Emans	1988/89
I/11.2	Cantatas for the 3d Sunday after Easter: BWV 12, 103, 146	Reinmar Emans	1989/89
I/12	Cantatas for the 4th Sunday after Easter to the Sunday after Ascension: BWV 166, 108, 86, 87, 37, 128, 43, 44, 183	Alfred Dürr	1960/60
I/13	Cantatas for Pentecost Sunday: BWV 172, 59, 174, 34	Dietrich Kilian	1959/60
I/14	Cantatas for Pentecost Monday and Tuesday: BWV 173, 68, 14, 184, 175	Alfred Dürr, Arthur Mendel	1962/63
I/15	Cantatas for Trinity and the Sunday after Trinity: BWV 165, 176, 129, 75, 20, 39, (194)	Alfred Dürr, Robert Freeman, James Webster	1967/68
I/16	Cantatas for the 2d and 3d Sunday after Trinity: BWV 76, 2, 21, 135	Robert Moreen, George S. Bozarth, Paul Brainard	1981/84
I/17.1	Cantatas for the 4th Sunday after Trinity: BWV 185, 24, 177	Yoshitake Kobayashi, Kirsten Beißwenger	1993/93
I/17.2	Cantatas for the 5th and 6th Sundays after Trinity: BWV 93, 88, 170, 9	Reinmar Emans	1993/93
I/18	Cantatas for the 7th and 8th Sundays after Trinity: BWV 54, 186, 107, 187, 136, 178, 45 (Anh. 1)	Alfred Dürr, Leo Treitler	1966/67
I/19	Cantatas for the 9th and 10th Sundays after Trinity: BWV 105, 94, 168, 46, 101, 102	Robert L. Marshall	1985/89

(cont'd)

Neue Bach-Ausgabe, *continued*

Ser. & Vol.	Contents (items in parentheses only in the critical reports)	Editor	Dates (music vol./critical report)
I/20	Cantatas for the 11th and 12th Sundays after Trinity: BWV 199, 179, 113, 69a, 137, 35	Klaus Hofmann, Ernest May	1986/85
I/21	Cantatas for the 13th and 14th Sundays after Trinity: BWV 77, 33, 164, 25, 78, 17	Werner Neumann	1958/59
I/22	Cantatas for the 15th Sunday after Trinity: BWV 138, 99, 51	Matthias Wendt	1987/88
I/23	Cantatas for the 16th and 17th Sundays after Trinity: BWV 161, 95, 8, 27, 148, 114, 47	Helmuth Osthoff, Rufus Hallmark	1982/84
I/24	Cantatas for the 18th and 19th Sundays after Trinity: BWV 96, 169, 48, 5, 56 (Anh. 2)	Matthias Wendt	1990/91
I/25	Cantatas for 20th and 21st Sundays after Trinity		
I/26	Cantatas for the 22d and 23d Sundays after Trinity: BWV 89, 115, 55, 163, 139, 52	Andreas Glöckner	1994/95
I/27	Cantatas for the 24th to 27th Sundays after Trinity: BWV 60, 26, 90, 116, 70, 140	Alfred Dürr	1968/68
I/28.1	Cantatas for Purification: BWV 83, 125, 82, 200 (157–58, 161)	Matthias Wendt, Uwe Wolf	1994/94
I/28.2	Cantatas for Visitation and Annunciation: BWV 1, 147, 10, (182)	Matthias Wendt, Uwe Wolf	1995/95
I/29	Cantatas for St. John: BWV 167, 7, 30	Frieder Rempp	1982/84

I/30	Cantatas for St. Michael: BWV 130, 19, 149, 50	Marianne Helms	1973/74
I/31	Cantatas for Reformation Day and organ consecration: BWV 79, 80b, 80, 194	Frieder Rempp	1987/88
I/32.1	Cantatas for the Mühlhausen and Leipzig town councils: BWV 71, 119, 193 (Anh. 192, Anh. 4)	Christine Fröde	1992/92
I/32.2	Cantatas for the Leipzig town council: BWV 29, 120, 69, (Anh. 3, Anh. 193)	Christine Fröde	1994/94
I/33	Cantatas for wedding services: BWV 196, 34a, 120a, 197, 195	Frederick Hudson	1958/58
I/34	Cantatas for various or unknown church services: BWV 106, 157, 131, 192, 117, 97, 100, 1045 (244a, Anh. 5, Anh. 15, 190a, 120b, Anh. 4a, 223)	Ryuichi Higuchi	1986/90
I/35	Cantatas for princes of Weimar, Weissenfels, and Köthen: BWV 208, 134a, 173a, (249a, 66a, Anh. 6–8, 184a, 194a, 36a)	Alfred Dürr	1963/64
I/36	Cantatas for Dresden nobility: BWV 213–14, 206, (Anh. 9, 193a, Anh. 11–12)	Werner Neumann	1963/62
I/37	Cantatas for Dresden nobility: BWV 207a, 215, (205a, 208a, Anh. 13)	Werner Neumann	1961/61
I/38	Cantatas for Leipzig University: BWV 205, 207, 198, 36b, (Anh. 20)	Werner Neumann	1960/60
I/39	Cantatas for Leipzig city and school, and music for aristocratic and bourgeois celebrations: BWV 36c, 30a, 210a, 212, (216a, Anh. 18–19, 249b, Anh. 10)	Werner Neumann	1975/77

(cont'd)

Neue Bach-Ausgabe, *continued*

Ser. & Vol.	Contents (items in parentheses only in the critical reports)	Editor	Dates (music vol./ critical report)
I/40	Cantatas for weddings and various secular occasions: BWV 202, 216, 210, 204, 201, 211, (*Auf, süß entzückende Gewalt*)	Werner Neumann	1969/70
I/41	Cantatas for various secular occasions		
II/1	*Mass in B Minor:* BWV 232	Friedrich Smend	1954/56
II/2	Masses and mass movements: BWV 234, 236, 235, 233, 233a, Anh. 26, 242, 237–38, (1081, Anh. 166)	Emil Platen, Marianne Helms	1978/82
II/3	*Magnificat* in D, in E-flat: BWV 243, 243a	Alfred Dürr	1955/55
II/4	*St. John Passion:* BWV 245	Arthur Mendel	1973/74
II/5	*St. Matthew Passion:* BWV 244; (*St. Mark Passion:* BWV 247)	Alfred Dürr	1972/74
II/5a	Facsimile of early version of *St. Matthew Passion:* BWV 244b	Alfred Dürr	1972
II/6	*Christmas Oratorio:* BWV 248	Walter Blankenburg, Alfred Dürr	1960/62
II/7	*Easter Oratorio:* BWV 249	Paul Brainard	1977/81
II/8	*Ascension Oratorio:* BWV 11	Paul Brainard	1978
II/8, rev. ed.	*Ascension Oratorio:* BWV 11	Paul Brainard	1983/87
II/9	Sanctus arrangements		
III/1	Motets: BWV 225–30, 118	Konrad Ameln	1965/67

III/2.1	Chorales and sacred lieder: BWV 250–52, Dietel chorales, Schemelli lieder	Frieder Rempp	1991/91
III/2.2	Chorales from C.P.E. Bach's printed collection, 1784–87	Frieder Rempp	1996/96
III/3	Sacred songs, etc.		
IV/1	*Orgelbüchlein*, Schübler chorales, Chorale partitas	Heinz-Harald Löhlein	1983/87
IV/2	Leipzig organ chorales	Hans Klotz	1958/57
IV/3	Individually transmitted organ chorales	Hans Klotz	1961/62
IV/4	Organ mass: *Clavier-Übung* III	Manfred Tessmer	1969/74
IV/5	Organ preludes, toccatas, fantasias, fugues I	Dietrich Kilian	1972/78–79 (3 vols., each for IV/5–6)
IV/6	Organ preludes, toccatas, fantasias, fugues II; early versions to and variants of I and II	Dietrich Kilian	1964/78–79 (3 vols., each for IV/5–6)
IV/7	Organ sonatas, misc. individual works	Dietrich Kilian	1984/88
IV/8	Organ concerto arrangements, organ trio arrangements	Karl Heller	1979/80
IV/9	Organ chorale settings		
V/1	Keyboard partitas: *Clavier-Übung* I	Richard Douglas Jones	1976/78
V/2	*Italian Concerto* and *French Overture: Clavier-Übung* II, BWV 831a; *Goldberg Variations: Clavier-Übung* IV, Fourteen Goldberg Canons	Walter Emery, Christoph Wolff	1977/81

(cont'd)

Neue Bach-Ausgabe, *continued*

Ser. & Vol.	Contents (items in parentheses only in the critical reports)	Editor	Dates (music vol./ critical report)
V/3	Two- and Three-part Inventions	Georg von Dadelsen	1970/
V/4	Music books for Anna Magdalena Bach of 1722 and 1725	Georg von Dadelsen	1957/57
V/5	Keyboard book for Wilhelm Friedemann Bach	Wolfgang Plath	1962/63
V/6.1	*Well-Tempered Clavier* I	Alfred Dürr	1989/89
V/6.2	*Well-Tempered Clavier* II; BWV 870a, 899–902	Alfred Dürr, critical report with Bettina Faulstich	1995/96
V/7	*English Suites*	Alfred Dürr	1979/81
V/8	*French Suites,* BWV 818–19, 818a–19a	Alfred Dürr	1980/82
V/9	Individually transmitted keyboard works I		
V/10	Individually transmitted keyboard works II, lute works	Hartwig Eichberg, Thomas Kohlhase	1976/82
V/11–12	Miscellaneous keyboard works		
VI/1	Sonatas and partitas for violin solo: BWV 1001–6; Six sonatas for harpsichord and violin: BWV 1014–19; sonatas: BWV 1021, 1023	Günter Hausswald, Rudolf Gerber	1958/58
VI/2	Cello suites: BWV 1007–12	Hans Eppstein	1988/90 and facsimile vol. 1991

VI/3	Flute partita and sonatas: BWV 1013, 1034–35, 1030, 1032; trio sonata: BWV 1039	Hans-Peter Schmitz; Alfred Dürr: Ergänzung zum kritischen Bericht BWV 1032, 1981	1963/63
VI/4	Viola da gamba sonatas: BWV 1027–29	Hans Eppstein	1984/89
VII/1	Orchestral suites: BWV 1066–69	Heinrich Besseler, Hans Grüss	1967/67
VII/2	Brandenburg Concertos: BWV 1046–51	Heinrich Besseler	1956/56
VII/2, supp.	Early version of Fifth Brandenburg Concerto: BWV 1050a	Alfred Dürr	1975
VII/3	Violin concertos: BWV 1041–43; Triple Concerto for flute, violin, and harpsichord: BWV 1044	Dietrich Kilian	1986/89
VII/4	Harpsichord concertos		
VII/5	Concertos for two harpsichords: BWV 1060–62, 1061a	Karl Heller, Hans-Joachim Schulze	1985/90
VII/6	Concertos for three and four harpsichords: BWV 1063–65	Rudolf Eller, Karl Heller	1975/76
VII/7	[supplementary volume] Reconstructions of concertos BWV 1052, 1055–56, 1060, 1064	Wilfried Fischer	1970/71
VIII/1	Canons: BWV 1072–78, 1086, Musical Offering: BWV 1079	Christoph Wolff	1974/76
VIII/2.1	Art of Fugue from the original edition: BWV 1080	Klaus Hofmann	1995/96
VIII/2.2	Art of Fugue from the autograph sources: BWV 1080	Klaus Hofmann	1995/96
IX/addenda/1	Catalogue of watermarks in Bach's original mss.—text	Wisso Weiss, Yoshitake Kobayashi	1985

(cont'd)

Neue Bach-Ausgabe, *continued*

Ser. & Vol.	*Contents* (items in parentheses only in the critical reports)	*Editor*	*Dates* (music vol./ critical report)
IX/add-enda/1	Catalogue of watermarks in Bach's original mss.—illustrations	Wisso Weiss, Yoshitake Kobayashi	1985
IX/add-enda/2	Bach's handwriting	Yoshitake Kobayashi	1989
IX/adden-da/3	Handwriting of Bach's copyists		

6.2.4 Other important editions

Nearly all modern editions (good and bad) of Bach's music have been derived not from early manuscripts but from collected works editions, usually the BG. The BWV and BC do sometimes list other modern editions than the BG and NBA, but only when these others have been based on direct study of the early sources. Whereas the collected works editions are designed primarily for scholars, other important modern editions are aimed primarily at performers—for example, they provide chordal realizations of the basso continuo lines.

For many Bach works and pieces by other composers in Bach's library, good practical editions based on independent scholarly evaluation of sources have been published by Hänssler-Verlag (now Carus-Verlag) in the
Stuttgarter Bach-Ausgaben. [with various series and subdivisions]

For several Bach instrumental works, good practical editions based on independent scholarly evaluation of sources have been jointly printed by various publishers in the series entitled
Wiener-Urtext Ausgaben.

7

Vocal music

7.1 Texts and librettists

7.1.1 Texts

The texts of Bach's vocal works are available in two forms: "original" sources (from Bach's time) and modern compilations.

Original texts, when they survive, provide valuable information about the composition and performance of the works, though for many of Bach's vocal compositions we have no original text sources and do not know the identity of the authors. Modern compilations are useful for getting an overview of a work's text, for seeing poetic texts in their verse forms, and for identifying biblical texts and chorale stanzas.

Original texts

Original text sources for Bach's vocal works are of several different kinds. A few are the texts from which Bach worked when composing: manuscript texts and those from printed collections (for example, those published by E. Neumeister). Some sources are related to the performance of Bach's music, such as the "Texte zur Leipziger Kirchenmusik," which contain cantata texts and were available to the Leipzig congregations. Other texts appear in collections published by their authors (for example, by Franck, Picander, and Ziegler), sometimes in revised versions that do not match Bach's setting exactly.

The surviving original text sources for Bach's vocal music are reproduced in facsimile in

Werner Neumann, ed. *Sämtliche von Johann Sebastian Bach vertonte Texte.* **Leipzig, 1974.**

The critical commentaries to volumes of the Neue Bach-Ausgabe often also include reproductions of original text sources.

A few original text sources have surfaced since the publication of Neumann's collection. The most important are reported in

Walter Blankenburg. "Eine neue Textquelle zu sieben Kantaten Johann Sebastian Bachs und achtzehn Kantaten Johann Ludwig Bachs." *BJ* 63 (1977): 7–25. [BWV 17, 39, 43, 45, 88, 102, 187]

Helmut K. Krausse. "Eine neue Quelle zu drei Kantatentexten Johann Sebastian Bachs." *BJ* 67 (1981): 7–22. [models for BWV 64, 69a and 77 by M. Johann Knauer]

Renate Steiger. "Actus tragicus und ars moriendi: Bachs Textvorlage für die Kantate 'Gottes Zeit ist die allerbeste Zeit' (BWV 106)." *Musik und Kirche* 59 (1989): 11–23. [possible model for BWV 106]

Hildegard Tiggemann. "Unbekannte Textdrucke zu drei Gelegenheitskantaten J.S. Bachs aus dem Jahre 1729." *BJ* 80 (1994): 7–22. [BWV 210a, "Der Herr ist freundlich" BWV deest, and "Vergnügende Flammen, verdoppelt die Macht" BWV deest]

Modern collections

Modern collections present the texts of Bach's vocal works in transcription, usually together with annotations of biblical and chorale sources. Note that there are sometimes conflicting readings among original editions, Bach's scores, and the original performing parts.

The standard collection of Bach's complete vocal texts, also containing facsimiles of all the original texts sources, is

Werner Neumann, ed. *Sämtliche von Johann Sebastian Bach vertonte Texte.* **Leipzig, 1974.**

A new collection is in preparation by Martin Petzoldt.

A computer-generated concordance of Bach's vocal texts, though hard to come by, is available in typescript in a few libraries:

Arthur Mendel. *Princeton Bach concordance.* **Princeton, 1979.**

Several text collections are devoted to Bach's cantatas. The first important compilation was

Rudolf Wustmann, ed. *Joh. Seb. Bachs Kantatentexte.* **Veröffentlichungen der Neuen Bachgesellschaft 14/1. Leipzig, 1913. 2d ed. Leipzig, 1967. 3d ed. Wiesbaden, 1982.**

This work is still useful because Wustmann had access to text sources that have since been lost, most importantly an early print of the so-called Picander-Jahrgang. The texts of the cantatas are also available in the expanded version of Alfred Dürr's invaluable guide:

Alfred Dürr. *Die Kantaten von Johann Sebastian Bach mit ihren Texten.* 5th ed. 2 vols. Munich and Cassel, 1985.

There are several English translations of the texts of Bach's cantatas. The most useful is

Texte zu den Kirchenkantaten von Johann Sebastian Bach / The texts to Johann Sebastian Bach's church cantatas. Translation by Z. Philip Ambrose. Neuhausen-Stuttgart, 1984.

This volume, connected with Helmuth Rilling's recordings of the cantatas, presents the original texts alongside ingenious translations that maintain the metrical organization and word order of the German originals.

The following two well-known books provide less literal singing translations of Bach's cantatas (and other vocal works in the second):

Charles Sanford Terry. *Joh. Seb. Bach: cantata texts, sacred and secular, with a reconstruction of the Leipzig liturgy of his period.* London, 1926.

Henry S. Drinker. *Texts of the choral works of Johann Sebastian Bach in English translation.* 4 vols. New York, 1942–43.

The following volume presents line-by-line English translations in German word order, together with biblical texts the author claims are referred to. (From the point of view of eighteenth-century theology, these should be used with caution; for more on biblical allusions in Bach's cantata librettos, see the literature in *7.1.3 Writings on vocal texts*).

Melvin P. Unger. *Handbook to Bach's sacred cantata texts: an interlinear translation with reference guide to biblical quotations and allusions.* Lanham, Md., 1996.

7.1.2 Librettists

Here we list literature on librettists and their connections to Bach. These authors and their works are also discussed in the general writings on Bach's texts cited below. For a list of these librettists' publications and which of Bach's pieces appear in them, see

Werner Neumann, ed. *Sämtliche von Johann Sebastian Bach vertonte Texte,* 509–12. Leipzig, 1974.

Salomo Franck (1659–1725)

Joshua Rifkin. "Franck, Salomo." *New Grove.*

Christian Friedrich Henrici [Picander] (1700–1764)

Paul Flossmann. "Picander (Christian Friedrich Henrici)." Ph.D. diss. University of Leipzig, 1899.

Joshua Rifkin. "Henrici, Christian Friedrich." *New Grove.*

Klaus Häfner. "Der Picander-Jahrgang." *BJ* 61 (1975): 70–113.

Klaus Häfner. "Picander, der Textdichter von Bachs viertem Kantaten-jahrgang: ein neuer Hinweis." *Die Musikforschung* 35 (1982): 156–62.

For the extensive literature on the question of whether Bach indeed set the complete Picander-Jahrgang to music and the related question of how many cantata cycles he composed, see *7.3.1 Cantatas.*

Christian Friedrich Hunold [Menantes] (1681–1721)

Friedrich Smend. *Bach in Köthen.* Berlin, 1951. Translated by John Page and edited and revised by Stephen Daw as *Bach in Köthen.* St. Louis, 1985.

George J. Buelow. "Hunold, Christian Friedrich." *New Grove.*

Georg Christian Lehms (1684–1717)

Elisabeth Noack. "Georg Christian Lehms, ein Textdichter Johann Sebastian Bachs." *BJ* 56 (1970): 7–18.

Joshua Rifkin. "Lehms, Georg Christian." *New Grove.*

Erdmann Neumeister (1671–1756)

Kerala Johnson Snyder. "Neumeister, Erdmann." *New Grove.*

Helmut K. Krausse. "Erdmann Neumeister und die Kantatentexte Johann Sebastian Bachs." *BJ* 72 (1986): 7–31.

Note that Neumeister's place as the "inventor" of the mixed-text-type libretto has been challenged; on compositions by Georg Caspar Schürmann in Meiningen from 1705, see
Konrad Küster. "Meininger Kantatentexte um Johann Ludwig Bach." *BJ* 73 (1987): 159–64.

Christiane Mariane von Ziegler (1695–1760)

Joshua Rifkin. "Ziegler, Christiane Mariane von." *New Grove.*

7.1.3 Writings on vocal texts

The principal large-scale studies of the texts of Bach's vocal music are

Luigi Ferdinando Tagliavini. *Studi sui testi delle cantate sacre di J.S. Bach.* **Padua, 1956.**

Ferdinand Zander. "Die Dichter der Kantatentexte Johann Sebastian Bachs: Untersuchungen zu ihrer Bestimmung." Ph.D. diss. University of Cologne, 1967; partial reprint as "Die Dichter der Kantatentexte Johann Sebastian Bachs: Untersuchungen zu ihrer Bestimmung." *BJ* 54 (1968): 9–64.

Harald Streck. *Die Verskunst in den poetischen Texten zu den Kantaten J.S. Bachs.* **Hamburg, 1971.**

The best source for information on the biblical content of Bach's church cantata librettos is

Ulrich Meyer. *Biblical quotation and allusion in the cantata libretti of Johann Sebastian Bach.* **Lanham, Md., 1997.**

On the text as Bach's compositional starting point, see

Paul Brainard. "The regulative and generative roles of verse in Bach's 'thematic' invention." In *Bach studies*, edited by Don O. Franklin, 54–74. Cambridge, 1989.

For literature on the texts of individual works, see the bibliographic entries in the BC under the subheading "Literatur/Text."

On Bach's texts, see also *11.2 Theological studies, 4.3.2 The liturgy,* and *7.2.8 Parody.*

7.2 All the vocal music

7.2.1 Overviews of Bach's vocal music

The most useful tools for locating vocal compositions and individual movements are the indexes at the end of the fourth volume of the BC; there are indexes of text incipits, works titles, genre designations, named characters, instrumental movements, and melodies quoted instrumentally. There is also an index of first lines of movements in

Werner Neumann, ed. *Sämtliche von Johann Sebastian Bach vertonte Texte.* **Leipzig, 1974.**

7.2.2 Chronologies of Bach's vocal music

A great deal of modern Bach scholarship has been concerned with the dating of Bach's vocal music and the revision of the chronology proposed by Philipp Spitta. The first comprehensive chronology of Bach's early cantatas is found in

> **Alfred Dürr.** *Studien über die frühen Kantaten Johann Sebastian Bachs.* 2d ed. Wiesbaden, 1977.

Dürr's volume, a revised version of a study first published in 1951, includes a hypothetical calendar of Bach's church cantata performances in Weimar. Important revisions to this chronology are presented in

> **Andreas Glöckner.** "Zur Chronologie der Weimarer Kantaten Johann Sebastian Bachs." *BJ* 71 (1985): 159–64.

A somewhat different chronology of Bach's Weimar cantatas is proposed in

> **Klaus Hofmann.** "Neue Überlegungen zu Bachs Weimarer Kantaten-Kalender." *BJ* 79 (1993): 9–29.

The following study establishes new datings of early vocal works on the basis of source studies:

> **Yoshitake Kobayashi.** "Quellenkundliche Überlegungen zur Chronologie der Weimarer Vokalwerke Bachs." In *Das Frühwerk Johann Sebastian Bachs: Kolloquium veranstaltet vom Institut für Musikwissenschaft der Universität Rostock 11.–13. September 1990,* edited by Karl Heller and Hans-Joachim Schulze, 290–310. Cologne, 1995.

The late 1950s saw the publication of two essential chronologies of Bach's Leipzig compositions based on source studies:

> **Alfred Dürr.** *Zur Chronologie der Leipziger Vokalwerke J.S. Bachs.* 2d ed. Cassel, 1976.

> **Georg von Dadelsen.** *Beiträge zur Chronologie der Werke Johann Sebastian Bachs.* Tübinger Bach-Studien 4/5. Trossingen, 1958.

Dürr's work, a revised version of a study first published in *BJ* 1957, includes a reconstructed calendar of Bach's performances in his Leipzig years, based largely on investigations of paper, copyists, and the grouping of cantatas into yearly cycles. Dadelsen's study, like Dürr's, presents a new chronology of Bach's Leipzig church music, based largely on the close study of Bach's handwriting and that of his copyists.

The findings of these studies by Dürr and Dadelsen are summarized in a chronological table of Bach's vocal music in the preface to

Gerhard Herz, ed. *Johann Sebastian Bach, Cantata no. 140: Wachet auf, ruft uns die Stimme.* **Norton Critical Score. New York, 1972.**

Numerous studies published since Dürr and Dadelsen's chronologies have corrected and expanded their findings. Among the most important for the vocal music is

Andreas Glöckner. "Neuerkenntnisse zu Johann Sebastian Bachs Aufführungskalender zwischen 1729 und 1735." *BJ* 67 (1981): 43–75.

For Bach's later years, the essential chronological study of Bach's composing and performing activities documented in original sources is

Yoshitake Kobayashi. "Zur Chronologie der Spätwerke Johann Sebastian Bachs: Kompositions- und Aufführungstätigkeit von 1736 bis 1750." *BJ* 74 (1988): 7–72.

7.2.3 Choruses

For literature on what constitutes a "chorus" in Bach's music, see *9.1 Vocal forces.*

An extremely influential analytical study of Bach's choruses that introduced the term "permutation fugue" to describe an important contrapuntal technique in Bach's early vocal music is

Werner Neumann. *J.S. Bachs Chorfuge: ein Beitrag zur Kompositionstechnik Bachs.* Leipzig, 1938. 2d ed. Bach-Studien 3. Leipzig, 1950. 3d ed. Leipzig, 1953.

On this topic see also

Norman Rubin. "'Fugue' as a delimiting concept in Bach's choruses: a gloss on Werner Neumann's 'J.S. Bachs Chorfuge.'" In *Studies in Renaissance and Baroque music in honor of Arthur Mendel,* edited by Robert L. Marshall, 195–208. Hackensack, 1974.

On the history of the permutation fugue, see

Paul Walker. "Die Entstehung der Permutationsfuge." *BJ* 75 (1989): 21–41. English version: "The origin of the permutation fugue." *Studies in the history of music.* Vol. 3, *The creative process,* 51–91. New York, 1993.

On choral settings of chorales, see

Emil Platen. "Untersuchungen zur Struktur der chorischen Choralbearbeitung Johann Sebastian Bachs." Ph.D. diss. University of Bonn, 1959.

On the historical context of Bach's settings of chorales (in choruses and other types of pieces), see

Friedhelm Krummacher. "Die Tradition in Bachs vokalen Choral-bearbeitungen." *Bach-Interpretationen,* edited by Martin Geck, 29–56. Göttingen, 1969.

On Bach's use of sixteenth-century counterpoint, see

Christoph Wolff. *Der Stile antico in der Musik Johann Sebastian Bachs: Studien zu Bachs Spätwerk.* Wiesbaden, 1968.

Many of the main points are summarized in

Christoph Wolff. "Bach and the tradition of the Palestrina style." In his *Bach: essays on his life and music,* 84–104. Cambridge, Mass., 1991.

On Bach's use of motet style in concerted vocal music, see

Daniel R. Melamed. *J.S. Bach and the German motet.* Cambridge, 1995.

7.2.4 Arias

The following work is a survey of a large group of Bach's arias:

Stephen A. Crist. "Aria forms in the vocal works of J.S. Bach, 1714–1724." Ph.D. diss. Brandeis University, 1988.

Crist's study is excerpted in

Stephen A. Crist. "Aria forms in the cantatas from Bach's first Leizpig *Jahrgang.*" In *Bach studies,* edited by Don O. Franklin, 36–53. Cambridge, 1989.

Two particularly good analytical studies of the musical material of Bach's arias are

Paul Brainard. "The aria and its ritornello: the question of 'dominance' in Bach." In *Bachiana et alia musicologica: Festschrift Alfred Dürr zum 65. Geburtstag am 3. März 1983,* edited by Wolfgang Rehm, 39–51. Cassel, 1983.

Paul Brainard. "The regulative and generative roles of verse in Bach's 'thematic' invention." In *Bach studies,* edited by Don O. Franklin, 54–74. Cambridge, 1989.

7.2.5 Ariosos and accompanied recitatives

The only systematic treatment is

Rebekka Bertling. *Das Arioso und das ariose Accompagnato im Vokal-werk Johann Sebastian Bachs.* Frankfurt, 1992.

7.2.6 Recitatives

The most extensive treatment of Bach's recitatives, displaying a somewhat rigid formalism, is

Hermann Melchert. "Das Rezitativ der Kirchenkantaten Joh. Seb. Bachs." Ph.D. diss. University of Frankfurt am Main, 1958. Substantially reprinted in *BJ* 45 (1958): 5–83.

On recitative accompaniment, see

Laurence Dreyfus. *Bach's continuo group: players and practices in his vocal works.* Cambridge, Mass., 1987.

7.2.7 Instrumentation in Bach's vocal music

For general works on Bach's instruments and instrumentation, see *9.2 Bach's instrumental forces* and *9.3 Instruments.*

Two studies important to the vocal music are

Ulrich Prinz. "Studien zum Instrumentarium Johann Sebastian Bachs mit besonderer Berücksichtigung der Kantaten." Ph.D. diss. University of Tübingen, 1979.

Laurence Dreyfus. *Bach's continuo group: players and practices in his vocal works.* Cambridge, Mass., 1987.

Prinz's study includes detailed lists of range and nomenclature for many of the instruments Bach used. Dreyfus's topics include the use of the harpsichord in sacred music, "double accompaniment" (organ and harpsichord together), the identity of various continuo instruments (bassoon, violone), and conventions of recitative accompaniment.

7.2.8 Parody

In Bach scholarship, "parody" refers to the process of retexting a piece of vocal music. A great deal has been written on Bach's parody procedure, both on technical aspects and on aesthetic significance. For a list of Bach movements related by parody, see the index of

Werner Neumann. *Handbuch der Kantaten Joh. Seb. Bachs.* 5th ed. Wiesbaden, 1984.

The history of scholarship on the Bach parody issue is summarized in

Hans-Joachim Schulze. "The parody process in Bach's music: an old problem reconsidered." *Bach* 20, no. 1 (1989): 7–21.

The most important general writings on parody are

Arnold Schering. "Über Bachs Parodieverfahren." *BJ* 18 (1921): 49–95.

Werner Neumann. "Über Ausmaß und Wesen des Bachschen Parodie-verfahrens." *BJ* 51 (1965): 63–85.

Friedrich Smend. *Bach in Köthen.* Berlin, 1951. Translated by John Page and edited and revised by Stephen Daw as *Bach in Köthen.* St. Louis, 1985.

Studies of parody in several individual works (the cantatas BWV 67, 136, 179, and Masses BWV 233–236) and discussions of the parody issue in general are found in

Renate Steiger, ed. *Parodie und Vorlage: zum Bachschen Parodie-verfahren und seiner Bedeutung für die Hermeneutik.* Internationale Arbeitsgemeinschaft für theologische Bachforschung Bulletin 2. Heidelberg, 1988.

The most famous pieces involved in parody include the *Christmas Oratorio,* the *St. Matthew Passion,* and the *Mass in B minor;* see the literature on these works.

7.2.9 Other topics in Bach's vocal music

Bach's vocal music is treated in many different kinds of studies. Here are a few particularly useful studies.

On dance meters and rhythms in the vocal works:

> **Doris Finke-Hecklinger.** *Tanzcharaktere in Johann Sebastian Bachs Vokalmusik.* **Tübinger Bach-Studien 6. Trossingen, 1970.**

On Bach's compositional process in the vocal works, with transcriptions of sketches and drafts:

> **Robert L. Marshall.** *The compositional process of J.S. Bach: a study of the autograph scores of the vocal works.* **2 vols. Princeton, 1972.**

On "tonal allegory," the representation of theological themes by harmonic organization:

> **Eric Chafe.** *Tonal allegory in the vocal music of J.S. Bach.* **Berkeley, 1991.**

7.3 Genres and individual vocal works

7.3.1 Cantatas

A handful of Bach's church cantatas date from his earliest professional years. To the extent that their purposes are known, they tend to be occasional works rather than cantatas for recurring feasts in the liturgical calendar. Approximately six pieces survive from this period.

Bach composed the bulk of his church cantatas during two periods when his duties required him to provide music for the regular Sunday liturgy. The first period was in Weimar, where after his appointment as Konzertmeister in 1714 he was required to write a cantata every four weeks. He apparently did not keep strictly to this schedule; there are gaps, and the exact chronology of these works is uncertain (see *7.2.2 Chronologies of Bach's vocal music*). Approximately 20 works are extant.

When Bach became Thomascantor and City Music Director in Leipzig, he was required to perform a cantata every Sunday. During his years in Leipzig, Bach composed several annual cycles of cantatas (Jahrgänge). A cycle consists of 65 to 70 cantatas for Sundays and feast days throughout the year; see *4.3 Liturgical context* for the organization of the church year.

The exact number of cycles Bach composed is uncertain, and has been the subject of much research. The obituary of Bach by C.P.E. Bach and Agricola (see *3.3.1 Primary and early biographies*) cites five cycles. Part or all of three cycles that Bach composed in his first years in Leipzig are known, representing more than 150 cantatas.

The designation of the Jahrgänge is a matter of interpretation. The church year is usually thought of as beginning with the First Sunday in Advent, but Bach took up his post and began cantata production in early summer, so his cantata cycles are usually reckoned as starting with the First Sunday after Trinity. For the most part, the cycles have been reconstructed based on liturgical and source evidence, but evidence of their transmission is also taken into account. One consequence is that several cantatas Bach composed later in his years in Leipzig are included in the earlier cycles—out of chronological order—because they were apparently meant to fill gaps.

For a tabular summary of the surviving cantata cycles, see the liturgical calendar in *4.3.1 The liturgical year*. Note that in Leipzig, no cantatas were performed during Advent (second through fourth Sundays) or during Lent (Invocavit through Palm Sunday, except when the feast of the Annunciation fell during this time); this was the so-called *tempus clausum*. For literature on the chronology of the cantatas, see *7.2.2 Chronologies of Bach's vocal music*.

The first Jahrgang began with "Die Elenden sollen essen" BWV 75 on 30 May 1723, the first Sunday after Trinity, and continued through "O heilges Geist- und Wasserbad" BWV 165 and the earlier version of "Höchsterwünschtes Freudenfest" BWV 194, both for Trinity Sunday, 4 June 1724. In this cycle, Bach presented revised versions of several of his Weimar cantatas and parodies of a few Köthen cantatas along with newly composed pieces.

The second Jahrgang began with "O Ewigkeit, du Donnerwort" BWV 20 on the first Sunday after Trinity, 11 June 1724 and continued through "Es ist ein trotzig und verzagt Ding" BWV 176 on Trinity Sunday, 27 May 1725. The texts of most of the cantatas in this cycle are based on hymns, and the cycle is frequently referred to as the "chorale Jahrgang." Actually, only the cantatas through Lent are constructed this way; for unknown reasons, Bach broke off the production of chorale cantatas. Most of the cantatas he composed for the remainder of the liturgical year were on librettos by Christiane Marianne von Ziegler. During his remaining 25 years in Leipzig, Bach composed several chorale-based cantatas that fill in some of the gaps in the cycle.

Bach apparently did not begin composing a third cycle immediately; the period after Trinity 1725 probably saw reperformances of extant cantatas. The third Jahrgang is usually considered as beginning with Advent 1725— or at least with Christmas Day 1725 ("Unser Mund sei voll Lachens" BWV 110), as no new cantata is known with certainty for the First Sunday in Advent, 2 December 1725. The end of this Jahrgang, in one view, comes with "Falsche Welt, dir trau ich nicht" BWV 52 for the Twenty-third Sunday after Trinity, 24 November 1726. During the year covered by this cycle, in addition to his own compositions, Bach performed 18 cantatas by his cousin Johann Ludwig Bach.

The best candidate for a fourth Jahrgang lies in the nine cantatas (plus one fragment) Bach composed c.1728–29 on texts by Christian Friedrich Henrici ("Picander"). The question of whether Bach actually composed the entire cycle of cantatas represented by the printed librettos has been much debated; see below (in this section) for literature. The identity of a putative fifth Jahrgang is even more mysterious; see below (in this section) for speculative literature.

The standard reference guide to Bach's cantatas is
Werner Neumann. *Handbuch der Kantaten Joh. Seb. Bachs.* 5th ed. Wiesbaden, 1984.

(This volume was first published as Veröffentlichungen der Neuen Bachgesellschaft 41–46/1. Leipzig, 1947. 2d ed. Leipzig, 1953. 3d ed. [reprint of 2d ed.] Wiesbaden, 1966 and Leipzig, 1966. 4th ed. Wiesbaden, 1971 and Leipzig, 1971. The 5th edition is a reprint of the 4th. The first edition also appeared in English as *Handbook of Joh. Seb. Bach's cantatas.* New York, 1947.)

Neumann presents a movement-by-movement outline of each cantata, giving scoring, vocal ranges, key, and basic musical organization. Text sources are identified, and there are references to relevant literature. The many indexes are particularly useful; they includes lists by date, liturgical occasion, librettist, type of chorale setting, chorale melodies, instrumentation, and arias by voice type and by obbligato scoring.

The best introduction to the cantatas and their historical and musical contexts is
Christoph Wolff, ed. *The world of the Bach cantatas.* 3 vols. New York, 1997– . Dutch, German, and Italian editions, Abcoude, 1995– .

The first volume covers pre-Leipzig church cantatas, the second volume secular works, and third volume Leipzig church cantatas. Each volume contains essays on Bach's activities, performance contexts of the works, librettos and librettists, musical types, and performance practice.

The most authoritative work-by-work treatment of the cantatas is
Alfred Dürr. *Die Kantaten von Johann Sebastian Bach.* 2 vols. Munich and Cassel, 1971. 2d ed. 1975. 3d ed. 1979. 4th ed. 1981.

The revised fifth edition of this work includes the complete texts of the cantatas:

Alfred Dürr. *Die Kantaten von Johann Sebastian Bach mit ihren Texten.* 5th ed. 2 vols. Munich and Cassel, 1985.

Dürr begins with an excellent introduction to the cantata before Bach, to the cantatas in general, and to performance issues. Each cantata is presented in movement-by-movement outline followed by a compact historical and analytical essay on the text and music.

There is no work-by-work study in English at the level of Dürr's, and it is difficult to recommend any of the surveys of Bach's cantatas. Most merely list and describe the movements, and some are based on greatly outdated information.

Much of the literature on the chronology of Bach's music is concerned with his cantatas; see *7.2.2 Chronologies of Bach's vocal music.* On the cantatas, see also *9.1 Vocal forces* and *4.3.2 The liturgy.*

The most important study of Bach's early cantatas, covering primarily pre-Weimar and Weimar works, is

Alfred Dürr. *Studien über die frühen Kantaten Johann Sebastian Bachs.* 2d ed. Wiesbaden, 1977.

Dürr's study is concerned entirely with Bach's music. A good introductory discussion of the early cantatas in the context of music by other composers is

Friedhelm Krummacher. "Bachs frühe Kantaten im Kontext der Tradition." *Die Musikforschung* 44 (1991): 9–32.

Bach's pre-Leipzig cantatas and issues surrounding them are discussed in the first volume of

Christoph Wolff, ed. *The world of the Bach cantatas.* 3 vols. New York, 1997– . Dutch, German, and Italian editions, Abcoude, 1995– .

For literature on the chronology of the early cantatas, see *7.2.2 Chronologies of Bach's vocal music.*

The so-called chorale cantatas, which make up Bach's second Leipzig cycle (1724–25), are each based on the text and music of a seasonally appropriate hymn. The outer movements are typically chorale settings; the inner movements are recitatives and arias whose texts paraphrase chorale verses. The author of the texts is unknown. See

Alfred Dürr. "Gedanken zu Bachs Choralkantaten." In *Johann Sebastian Bach*, edited by Walter Blankenburg, 507–17. *Wege der Forschung* 170. Darmstadt, 1970. In Dürr, *Im Mittelpunkt Bach: ausgewählte Aufsätze und Vorträge*, 126–32. Cassel, 1988. Translated as "Bach's chorale cantatas." In *Cantors at the crossroads: essays on church music in honor of Walter E. Buszin*, edited by Johannes Riedel, 111–20. St. Louis, 1967.

Renate Steiger, ed. *Johann Sebastian Bachs Choralkantaten als Choral-Bearbeitungen*. Internationale Arbeitsgemeinschaft für Theologische Bachforschung Bulletin 3. Heidelberg, 1991.

Friedhelm Krummacher. *Bachs Zyklus der Choralkantaten: Aufgaben und Lösungen*. Göttingen, 1995.

On the hymns themselves, see *7.3.6 Four-part chorales*.

The obituary of J.S. Bach published by Lorenz Mizler refers to five annual cycles of church cantatas. Only three cycles can be more or less fully accounted for; the question of the existence and fate of the putative fourth and fifth cycles has occupied Bach scholarship and been extensively debated in print. See *5.2.1 Bach's estate and its division* and *7.2.2 Chronologies of Bach's vocal music*. On specific topics:

On Mizler's report:

William H. Scheide. "Ist Mizlers Bericht über Bachs Kantaten korrekt?" *Die Musikforschung* 14 (1961): 60–63.

Alfred Dürr. "Wieviele Kantatenjahrgänge hat Bach komponiert? Eine Entgegnung." *Die Musikforschung* 14 (1961): 192–95.

William H. Scheide. "Nochmals Mizlers Kantatenbericht—Eine Erwiderung." *Die Musikforschung* 14 (1961): 423–27.

On the question of whether the so-called Picander-Jahrgang represents the fourth annual cycle:

Klaus Häfner. "Der Picander-Jahrgang." *BJ* 61 (1975): 70–113.

Walter Blankenburg. "Die Bachforschung seit etwa 1965." *Acta musicologica* 50 (1978): 93–154. [especially 104ff]

William H. Scheide. "Bach und der Picander-Jahrgang—Eine Erwiderung." *BJ* 66 (1980): 47–51.

Klaus Häfner. "Picander, der Textdichter von Bachs viertem Kantatenjahrgang: ein neuer Hinweis." *Die Musikforschung* 35 (1982): 156–62.

William H. Scheide. "Eindeutigkeit und Mehrdeutigkeit in Picanders Kantatenjahrgangs—Vorbemerkung und im Werkverzeichnis des Nekrologs auf Johann Sebastian Bach." *BJ* 69 (1983): 109–13.

Klaus Häfner. *Aspekte des Parodieverfahrens bei Johann Sebastian Bach: Beiträge zur Wiederentdeckung verschollener Vokalwerke.* Laaber, 1987.

On the identity of the fifth cycle:

Christoph Wolff. "Wo blieb Bachs fünfter Kantatenjahrgang?" *BJ* 68 (1982): 151–52.

Alfred Dürr. "Noch einmal: wo blieb Bachs fünfter Kantatenjahrgang?" *BJ* 72 (1986): 121–22.

Bach's secular cantatas are discussed in the second volume of

Christoph Wolff, ed. *The world of the Bach cantatas.* 3 vols. New York, 1997– . Dutch, German, and Italian editions, Abcoude, 1995– .

Many of the secular cantatas are involved in parody; see *7.2.8 Parody.*

Here we list literature in English on several famous church cantatas.

"Christ lag in Todesbanden" BWV 4

Gerhard Herz, ed. *Bach Cantata no. 4: Christ lag in Todesbanden.* Norton Critical Score. New York, 1967.

"Jesu, der du meine Seele" BWV 78

Robert L. Marshall. "On Bach's universality." In his *The music of Johann Sebastian Bach: the sources, the style, the significance,* 65–79. New York, 1989.

"Ein feste Burg ist unser Gott" BWV 80

Christoph Wolff. "Bach's cantata *Ein feste Burg:* history and performance practice." *American Choral Review* 24, nos. 2–3 (1982): 27–38.

"Herr, gehe nicht ins Gericht" BWV 105

Robert L. Marshall. "The autograph score of *Herr, gehe nicht ins Gericht,* BWV 105." In his *The music of Johann Sebastian Bach: the sources, the style, the significance,* 131–42. New York, 1989.

This essay traces the genesis of the cantata from Bach's autograph score.

"Wachet auf, ruft uns die Stimme" BWV 140

Gerhard Herz, ed. *Johann Sebastian Bach, Cantata no. 140: Wachet auf, ruft uns die Stimme.* **Norton Critical Score. New York, 1972.**

7.3.2 Passions

In Leipzig, Bach performed a concerted passion each Good Friday at Vespers. His passion performances in his first years there were:

Year	Work (* = 1st performance)	Church	
1724	* *St. John* BWV 245 (1st version)	St. Nicholas	
1725	*St. John* BWV 245 (2d version)		St. Thomas
1726	R. Keiser, *St. Mark*	St. Nicholas	
1727	* *St. Matthew* BWV 244		St. Thomas
1728	?	St. Nicholas	
1729	*St. Matthew* BWV 244		St. Thomas
1730	Anon., *St. Luke* BWV 246/Anh. II 30	St. Nicholas	
1731	* *St. Mark* BWV 247 [lost]		St. Thomas
1732	*St. John* BWV 245 (3d version)	?	
1733	[mourning period—no concerted passion]		
1734	?		
1735	?		
1736	*St. Matthew* BWV 244 (rev. version)		St. Thomas

On Bach's passions in the Leipzig liturgy for Good Friday, see *4.3.2 The liturgy* and see

Robin A. Leaver. "The mature vocal works and their theological and liturgical context." In *The Cambridge companion to Bach,* **edited by John Butt, 86–122. Cambridge, 1997.**

On the passion music by other composers connected to Bach, see, in general:

Andreas Glöckner. "Johann Sebastian Bachs Aufführungen zeitgenössischer Passionsmusiken." *BJ* 63 (1977): 75–119.

Andreas Glöckner. "Bach and the passion music of his contemporaries." *Musical Times* 116 (1975): 613–16.

On individual works, see the entries for some of these works in the BC (work groups D and X) and the tools cited in *4.2 Bach's library.*

C.P.E. Bach's obituary of his father mentions five passion settings, though only two survive. In addition, there is evidence that at least one large movement used both in the *St. John Passion* and *St. Matthew Passion* predates those works, and some scholars believe that Bach wrote a (lost) passion in Weimar. The early history of Bach's passion settings has thus been an important research topic. See

Alfred Dürr. "Zu den verschollenen Passionen Bachs." *BJ* 38 (1949/50): 81–99.

Arthur Mendel. "Traces of the pre-history of Bach's St. John and St. Matthew Passions." In *Festschrift Otto Erich Deutsch*, edited by Walter Gerstenberg et al., 31–48. Cassel, 1963.

Arthur Mendel. "More on the Weimar origin of Bach's *O Mensch, bewein."* *Journal of the American Musicological Society* 17 (1964): 203–6.

Recent essays on Bach's passion music can be found in

Hans-Joachim Schulze, Ulrich Leisinger and Peter Wollny, eds. *Passionsmusiken im Umfeld Johann Sebastian Bachs / Bach unter den Diktaturen, 1933–1945 und 1945–1989.* **Leipziger Beiträge zur Bachforschung 1. Hildesheim, 1995.**

The two most important performance practice issues in the passions concern the staffing and execution of the continuo line, and the number of performers (especially on the vocal parts). For literature, see *7.2.7 Instrumentation in Bach's vocal music* and *9.1 Vocal forces*.

St. Matthew Passion *BWV 244*

A useful survey:
Emil Platen. *Die Matthäus-Passion von Johann Sebastian Bach: Entstehung, Werkbeschreibung, Rezeption.* **Munich and Cassel, 1991.**

For essays on diverse topics, see
Ulrich Prinz, ed. *Johann Sebastian Bach, Matthäus-Passion, BWV 244: Vorträge der Sommerakademie J.S. Bach 1985.* **Stuttgart, 1990.**

The dating of the *St. Matthew Passion* and its parody relationship to the so-called Köthen Funeral Music have been much debated. Rifkin's date of 1727 and the priority of the *St. Matthew Passion* are now generally accepted by scholars. The basic literature is

Detlev Gojowy. "Zur Frage der Köthener Trauermusik und der Matthäuspassion." *BJ* 51 (1965): 86–134.

Paul Brainard. "Bach's parody procedure and the St. Matthew Passion." *Journal of the American Musicological Society* 22 (1969): 241–60.

Joshua Rifkin. "The chronology of Bach's Saint Matthew Passion." *Musical Quarterly* 61 (1975): 360–87.

See also *7.2.8 Parody.*

On the relationship between theology and music, see
Eric Chafe. "J.S. Bach's *St. Matthew Passion:* aspects of planning, structure and chronology." *Journal of the American Musicological Society* 35 (1982): 49–114.

Eric Chafe. *Tonal allegory in the vocal music of J.S. Bach.* Berkeley, 1991.

A performer's guide to the work by a leading conductor:
Helmuth Rilling. *Johann Sebastian Bach, Matthäus-Passion: Einführung und Studienanleitung.* Frankfurt, 1975. Translated by Kenneth Nafziger as *Johann Sebastian Bach, St. Matthew Passion: introduction and instructions for study.* Frankfurt, 1976.

On the nineteenth-century revival of the work, including the 1829 Berlin Sing-Akademie performance under Felix Mendelssohn, see
Martin Geck. *Die Wiederentdeckung der Matthäuspassion im 19. Jahrhundert: die zeitgenössischen Dokumente und ihre ideengeschichtliche Deutung.* Regensburg, 1967.

Barbara David Wright. "Johann Sebastian Bach's *Matthäus-Passion:* a performance history 1829–1854." Ph.D. diss. University of Michigan, 1983.

St. John Passion *BWV 245*

Two useful surveys:
Alfred Dürr. *Die Johannes-Passion von Johann Sebastian Bach: Entstehung, Überlieferung, Werkeinführung.* Munich and Cassel, 1988.

Martin Geck. *Johann Sebastian Bach: Johannespassion BWV 245.* Munich, 1991.

For essays on diverse topics, see
Ulrich Prinz, ed. *Johann Sebastian Bach, Johannes-Passion, BWV 245: Vorträge des Meisterkurses 1986 und der Sommerakademie J.S. Bach 1990.* Stuttgart, 1993.

On the relationship between theology and music, see
Eric Chafe. "Key structure and tonal allegory in the Passions of J.S. Bach: an introduction." *Current Musicology* 31 (1981): 39–54.

Eric Chafe. *Tonal allegory in the vocal music of J.S. Bach.* Berkeley, 1991.

Michael Marissen. *Lutheranism, anti-Judaism, and Bach's St. John Passion.* New York, 1998.

St. Mark Passion *BWV 247*

The text of this work survives, as do several parodied movements (mostly from the *Trauer-Ode* BWV 198) and probably several chorales, but most of the score is lost. All "reconstructions," whether by putative parodies, the use of music from Reinhard Keiser's setting, or free composition by the reconstructor, should be treated with caution.

The history of scholarship on the *St. Mark Passion* is summarized in the following study, which takes an overly optimistic view of the possibility of reconstructing the work.

Gustav Adolf Theill. *Die Markuspassion von Joh. Seb. Bach (BWV 247): Entstehung—Vergessen—Wiederentdeckung.* 2d ed. Steinfeld, 1981.

7.3.3 Oratorios

Christmas Oratorio *BWV 248*

There are two introductory volumes devoted to the *Christmas Oratorio:*
Walter Blankenburg. *Das Weihnachts-Oratorium von Johann Sebastian Bach.* Cassel, 1982.

Alfred Dürr. *Johann Sebastian Bach: Weihnachts-Oratorium BWV 248.* Munich, 1967.

On liturgical considerations, see
Robin A. Leaver. "The mature vocal works and their theological and liturgical context." In *The Cambridge companion to Bach,* edited by **John Butt, 86–122. Cambridge, 1997.**

The *Christmas Oratorio* is made up of six cantatas, so information can also be found in the general literature on cantatas.

Most of the concerted movements in the *Christmas Oratorio* are parodies of movements from secular cantatas. The work thus figures prominently in writings on parody; see *7.2.8 Parody*.

Other oratorios

The *Easter Oratorio* BWV 249 and the *Ascension Oratorio* BWV 11 have often been treated as cantatas; some discussions of them will be found in the cantata literature.

7.3.4 Latin works

On the role of Masses, Mass movements, and the Magnificat in the liturgy, see *4.3.2 The Liturgy* and see

Robin A. Leaver. "The mature vocal works and their theological and liturgical context." In *The Cambridge companion to Bach*, edited by John Butt, 86–122. Cambridge, 1997.

Mass movements

Much of the literature on Bach's individual Mass movements, principally Kyrie/Gloria settings and Sanctus settings, concerns parody and the place of Latin Ordinary movements in the liturgy. See *7.2.8 Parody* and *4.3.2 The liturgy*.

For literature on the Kyrie and Gloria that became the first part of the *Mass in B minor*, see below on that Mass.

A large proportion of music by other composers Bach performed consists of Mass movements; see *4.2 Bach's library*.

Mass in B minor *BWV 232*

The literature on the *Mass in B minor* is extensive. Recent introductions with summaries of scholarship and references to other literature are

John Butt. *Bach: Mass in B Minor*. Cambridge, 1991.

George Stauffer. *Bach: Mass in B Minor*. New York, 1997.

Another introduction to the work is

Walter Blankenburg. *Einführung in Bachs h-moll-Messe BWV 232*. 3d ed. Cassel, 1974.

A particularly useful essay on scholarship on the Mass is

Hans-Joachim Schulze. "The B minor Mass—perpetual touchstone for Bach research." In *Bach, Handel, Scarlatti: tercentenary essays*, edited by Peter Williams, 311–20. Cambridge, 1985.

A good introduction to the autograph score and issues it raises is
Robert L. Marshall. "Beobachtungen am Autograph der h-moll-Messe: zum Kompositionsprozeß J.S. Bachs." *Musik und Kirche* 50 (1980): 230–39. English translation as "The Mass in B Minor: the autograph scores and the compositional process." In Marshall, *The music of Johann Sebastian Bach: the sources, the style, the significance,* 175–89. New York, 1989.

Yoshitake Kobayashi's dating of the Mass as probably Bach's last work is his starting point for the following essay on the significance of the work:
Yoshitake Kobayashi. "Die Universalität in Bachs h-moll-Messe: ein Beitrag zum Bach-Bild der letzten Lebensjahre." *Musik und Kirche* 57 (1987): 9–24; Translated as "Universality in Bach's B Minor Mass: a portrait of Bach in his final years." *Bach* 24, no. 2 (1993): 3–25.

A guide to the work by a leading conductor:
Helmuth Rilling. *Johann Sebastian Bachs h-Moll-Messe.* Neuhausen-Stuttgart, 1979. 2d ed. Neuhausen-Stuttgart, 1986. First ed. translated by Gordon Paine as *Johann Sebastian Bach's B-minor mass.* Princeton, 1984.

A level-headed survey of what is known about parodied movements in the Mass is
Alfred Dürr. "Zur Parodiefrage in Bachs h-moll-Messe: eine Bestands-aufnahme." *Die Musikforschung* 45 (1992): 117–38.

The Mass has also figured in debates about the performance practice of Bach's vocal music; see *9.1 Vocal forces.*

Magnificat *BWV 243a and 243*

The best introduction to the compositional history of the two versions of the *Magnificat* is
Robert L. Marshall. "On the origin of Bach's Magnificat: a Lutheran composer's challenge." In *Bach studies,* edited by Don O. Franklin, 3–17. Cambridge, 1989. Also in Marshall, *The music of Johann Sebastian Bach: the sources, the style, the significance,* 161–73. New York, 1989.

The repertorial context of the *Magnificat* is discussed in
Robert Cammarota. "The repertoire of Magnificats in Leipzig at the time of J.S. Bach: a study of the manuscript sources." Ph.D. diss. New York University, 1986.

7.3.5 Motets

The following volume discusses authenticity, chronology, performance practice, musical style, and the compositional history of Bach's motets:

Daniel R. Melamed. *J.S. Bach and the German motet.* Cambridge, 1995.

The most extensive analytical discussion of Bach's motets is

Friedhelm Krummacher. "Textauslegung und Satzstruktur in J.S. Bachs Motetten." *BJ* 60 (1974): 5–43.

Much of the earlier literature on the motets, especially concerning their dating and purpose, is speculative and should be used with caution.

7.3.6 Four-part chorales

Bach's four-part chorales are transmitted both as parts of larger works and in collections probably associated with Bach's teaching. Some chorales thus have BWV numbers in the range that includes cantatas, oratorios, and the like (BWV 1–249), others in the range covering independent chorales (BWV 250–438).

The best basic resource for finding chorales is work group F of the BC. Each entry (F1–F213) corresponds to a distinct chorale melody; sub-entries list each four-part setting, whether it appears in a larger work or is transmitted independently. The BWV provides an alphabetical index (p. 460ff.) of text incipits, with BWV numbers and cross references to important printed editions.

To identify a chorale stanza in a vocal work, look up its first line in the resources listed under "Modern collections" in *7.1.1 Texts*. Keep in mind that a given tune was often associated with more than one text, and that each chorale text in turn has many stanzas. A complete citation of a chorale will usually tell which stanza it uses and how many stanzas there are altogether, and identify the author of the text, the date of its first publication, and the composer of the melody. The melody will often be indentified by its number in Zahn's compilation; see below (in this section).

On the early collections of Bach's chorales see

Friedrich Smend. "Zu den ältesten Sammlungen der vierstimmigen Choräle J.S. Bachs." *BJ* 52 (1966): 5–40. Reprinted in Smend. *Bach-*

Studien: gesammelte Reden und Aufsätze, edited by Christoph Wolff, 237–69. Cassel, 1969.

The most important manuscript source is Musikbibliothek der Stadt Leipzig Ms. R 18, copied by Bach's student Johann Ludwig Dietel from Bach's original performing materials. On this collection, whose chorales have since been published in NBA III/2.1, see

Hans-Joachim Schulze. "'150 Stück von den Bachischen Erben': zur Überlieferung der vierstimmigen Choräle Johann Sebastian Bachs." *BJ* 69 (1983): 81–100.

On the printed editions of Bach's chorales, see

Gerd Wachowski. "Die vierstimmigen Choräle Johann Sebastian Bachs: Untersuchungen zu den Druckausgaben von 1765 bis 1932 und zur Frage der Authentizität." *BJ* 69 (1983): 51–79.

On Bach's compositional process in the chorales, see

Robert L. Marshall. "How J.S. Bach composed four-part chorales." *Musical Quarterly* 56 (1970): 198–220.

Robert L. Marshall. *The compositional process of J.S. Bach: a study of the autograph scores of the vocal works.* 2 vols. Princeton, 1972.

For English translations of certain chorales, see

Mark S. Bighley. *The Lutheran chorales in the organ works of J.S. Bach.* St. Louis, 1986.

This volume contains translations of all the stanzas of 111 chorales that Bach used in his organ music. These translations are particularly useful for the study of the chorale cantatas.

For a convenient way of finding Bach's multiple harmonizations of chorale melodies, see

178 chorale harmonizations of Joh. Seb. Bach: a comparative edition for study, edited by Donald Martino. Rev. ed. Newton, Mass., 1985.

Texts of every chorale from the earliest repertory to the beginning of the seventeenth century are found in

Philipp Wackernagel. *Das deutsche Kirchenlied von der ältesten Zeit bis zu Anfang des XVII. Jahrhunderts.* 5 vols. Leipzig, 1864–77.

Chorales from the seventeenth century are covered in

Albert Fischer and W. Tümpel. *Das deutsche evangelische Kirchenlied des 17. Jahrhunderts.* 6 vols. Gütersloh, 1904–16.

Chorale melodies and their variants, organized by verse form, are collected in

Johannes Zahn. *Die Melodien der deutschen evangelischen Kirchenlieder.* 6 vols. Gütersloh, 1889–93.

This work is being superseded by

Joachim Stalmann, ed. *Das deutsche Kirchenlied: kritische Gesamtausgabe der Melodien.* Cassel, 1993– .

8

Instrumental music

8.1 All the instrumental music

8.1.1 General topics in Bach's instrumental music

There are no published overviews of Bach's instrumental music. For a wide-ranging discussion of Bach's composition of instrumental music, including close readings of selected works, see

Laurence Dreyfus. *Bach and the patterns of invention.* Cambridge, Mass., 1996.

8.1.2 Genres of Bach's instrumental music

The most far-reaching study of Bach's concerto style is

Laurence Dreyfus. "J.S. Bach's concerto ritornellos and the question of invention." *Musical Quarterly* 71 (1985): 327–58. Rev. as "The ideal ritornello." In his *Bach and the patterns of invention,* 59–102. Cambridge, Mass., 1996.

For a detailed survey of how Vivaldi's concerto style affected Bach's instrumental composition in various genres, see

Hans-Günter Klein. *Der Einfluss der Vivaldischen Konzertform im Instrumentalwerk Johann Sebastian Bachs.* Strasbourg, 1970.

See also *10.2 Bach and the music of other composers.*

The context of Bach's sonatas in concerto style (*Sonaten auf Concertenart*) is explored in

Jeanne R. Swack. "On the origins of the *Sonate auf Concertenart.*" *Journal of the American Musicological Society* 46 (1993): 369–414.

For a study of sonatas in various scorings, see

Hans Eppstein. *Studien über J.S. Bachs Sonaten für ein Melodie-instrument und obligates Cembalo.* Uppsala, 1966.

For a survey of chorale preludes, see

Ernest May. "The types, uses, and historical position of Bach's organ chorales." In *J.S. Bach as organist: his instruments, music, and performance practices,* edited by George Stauffer and Ernest May, 81–101. Bloomington, 1986.

Concerning Bach's preludes, see

Siegfried Hermelink. "Das Präludium in Bachs Klaviermusik." *Jahrbuch des Staatlichen Instituts für Musikforschung Preußischer Kulturbesitz, 1976,* 7–80. Berlin, 1977.

George B. Stauffer. *The organ preludes of Johann Sebastian Bach.* Ann Arbor, 1980.

On the relationships between the concepts "form," "genre," and "fugue," see

Laurence Dreyfus. "Matters of kind: genre and subgenre in Bach's *Well-Tempered Clavier,* Book I." In *A Bach tribute: essays in honor of William H. Scheide,* edited by Paul Brainard and Ray Robinson, 101–19. Cassel, 1993. Rev. as "Matters of kind." In Dreyfus. *Bach and the patterns of invention,* 135–68. Cambridge, Mass., 1996.

For more concerning Bach's instrumental fugues, see

Elke Krüger. *Stilistische Untersuchungen zu ausgewählten frühen Klavierfugen Johann Sebastian Bachs.* Hamburg, 1970.

George Stauffer. "Fugue types in Bach's free organ works." In *J.S. Bach as organist: his instruments, music, and performance practices,* edited by George Stauffer and Ernest May, 133–56. Bloomington, 1986.

Werner Breig. "Versuch einer Theorie der Bachschen Orgelfuge." *Die Musikforschung* 48 (1995): 14–52.

8.1.3 *Other topics in Bach's instrumental music*

Because virtually no composing scores survive, issues of chronology are much more vexing for Bach's instrumental works than for his vocal works. For studies that consider various genres, see

Christoph Wolff. "Bach's Leipzig chamber music." *Early Music* 13 (1985): 165–75. Rev. in his *Bach: essays on his life and music,* 223–38. Cambridge, Mass. 1991.

Martin Geck. "Köthen oder Leipzig? Zur Datierung der nur in Leipziger Quellen erhaltenen Orchesterwerke Johann Sebastian Bachs." *Die Musikforschung* 47 (1994): 17–24.

There are also questions about the extent of Bach's original output. For two different views on this subject, see

Christoph Wolff. "Die Orchesterwerke J.S. Bachs: grundsätzliche Erwägungen zu Repertoire, Überlieferung und Chronologie." In *Bachs Orchesterwerke: Bericht über das 1. Dortmunder Bach-Symposion im Januar 1996,* edited by Martin Geck and Werner Breig. Dortmund, forthcoming.

Joshua Rifkin. "Verlorene Quellen, verlorene Werke: Miszellen zu Bachs Instrumentalkomposition." In *Bachs Orchesterwerke: Bericht über das 1. Dortmunder Bach-Symposion im Januar 1996,* edited by Martin Geck and Werner Breig. Dortmund, forthcoming.

Some of Bach's lost instrumental music may survive as arrangements in his vocal music. For a speculative exploration of this issue, see

Walter F. Kindermann. *Wiedergewonnene Schwesterwerke der Brandenburgischen Konzerte Johann Sebastian Bachs.* Hofheim am Taunus, 1969.

Many of Bach's arrangements of his own works survive. They are studied in meticulous detail in

Ulrich Siegele. *Kompositionsweise und Bearbeitungstechnik in der Instrumentalmusik Johann Sebastian Bachs.* Neuhausen-Stuttgart, 1975.

Considerable attention has been paid to the disposition (tonal orderings and scoring layouts) of Bach's instrumental collections. The best place to start is

Christoph Wolff. "Ordnungsprinzipien in den Originaldrucken Bachscher Werke." In *Bach-Interpretationen,* edited by Martin Geck, 144–67. Göttingen, 1969. Revised version translated by Alfred Mann as "Principles of design and order in Bach's original editions." In Wolff., *Bach: essays on his life and music,* 340–58. Cambridge, Mass., 1991.

8.2 Genres and individual instrumental works

8.2.1 Solo organ

The most comprehensive treatment of all aspects of the repertory is the excellent study

Peter Williams. *The organ music of J.S. Bach.* 3 vols. Cambridge, 1980–84. Vol I: *Preludes, toccatas, fantasias, fugues, sonatas, concertos and miscellaneous pieces (BWV 525–98, 802–5, etc).* 1980. Vol. II: *Works based on chorales (BWV 599–771 etc.).* 1980. Vol. III: *A background.* 1984.

Be sure to notice the "Additions and corrections to volumes I and II" in vol. III, pp. 255–86.

Important additional material can be found in

George Stauffer and Ernest May, eds. *J.S. Bach as organist: his instruments, music, and performance practices.* Bloomington, 1986.

For discussion of the Neumeister chorales (a collection not known before the Williams and Stauffer books were published), see

Christoph Wolff. "Zur Problematik der Chronologie und Stilentwicklung des Bachschen Frühwerkes, insbesondere zur musikalischen Vorgeschichte des Orgelbüchleins." In *Bericht über die wissenschaftliche Konferenz zum V. internationalen Bachfest der DDR in Verbindung mit dem 60. Bachfest der Neuen Bachgesellschaft [Leipzig 1985]*, edited by Winfried Hoffmann and Armin Schneiderheinze, 449–55. Leipzig, 1988. Translated by Alfred Mann as "Chronology and style in the early works: a background for the Orgel-Büchlein." In Wolff, *Bach: essays on his life and music*, 297–305. Cambridge, Mass., 1991.

Christoph Wolff. "The Neumeister collection of chorale preludes from the Bach circle." In his *Bach: essays on his life and music*, 107–27. Cambridge, Mass., 1991

Alfred Dürr. "Kein Meister fällt vom Himmel: zu Johann Sebastian Bachs Orgelchorälen der Neumeister-Sammlung." *Musica* 40 (1986): 309–12.

Russell Stinson. "Some thoughts on Bach's Neumeister chorales." *Journal of Musicology* 11 (1993): 455–77.

For a recent study of the perennial question of authorship of the celebrated Toccata and Fugue in D minor, see

Rolf Dietrich Claus. *Zur Echtheit von Toccata und Fuge d-moll BWV 565.* Cologne, 1995.

8.2.2 Other solo keyboard

For a quick survey of the repertory, see
> Robert L. Marshall. "Johann Sebastian Bach." In *Eighteenth-century keyboard music,* edited by Robert L. Marshall, 68–123. New York, 1994.

The most comprehensive treatment of all aspects of Bach's keyboard music is the excellent study
> David Schulenberg. *The keyboard music of J.S. Bach.* New York, 1992.

"Solo keyboard" refers primarily to music for harpsichord but also for all other instruments without pedals encompassed by the term "clavier" (that is, clavichord, organ "manualiter" [manuals only], and fortepiano). On this question of what Bach meant by "clavier," see
> Robert L. Marshall. "Organ or 'Klavier'? Instrumental prescriptions in the sources of Bach's keyboard works." In *J.S. Bach as organist: his instruments, music, and performance practices,* edited by George Stauffer and Ernest May, 212–39. Bloomington, 1986. Rev. in Marshall, *The music of Johann Sebastian Bach: the sources, the style, the significance,* 271–93. New York, 1989.

8.2.3 Other solo works

A performer's survey of Bach's solo repertory for violin, cello, lute, and flute is provided by
> Hans Vogt. *Johann Sebastian Bachs Kammermusik: Voraussetzungen, Analysen, Einzelwerke.* Stuttgart, 1981. Translated by Kenn Johnson as *Johann Sebastian Bach's chamber music: background, analyses, individual works.* Portland, 1988.

On chronological and other issues surrounding the solo string music, see
> Hans Eppstein. "Chronologieprobleme in Johann Sebastian Bachs Suiten für Soloinstrumente." *BJ* 62 (1976): 35–57.

> Georg von Dadelsen. "Bach, der Violinist: Anmerkungen zu den Soli für Violine und für Violoncello." Beiträge zur Bachforschung 9/10 (1991): 70–76.

A stylistic survey of the solo violin works is

Günter Hausswald. "Zur Stilistik von Johann Sebastian Bachs Sonaten und Partiten für Violine allein." *Archiv für Musikwissenschaft* 14 (1957): 304–23.

For a study of their early versions, see
Russell Stinson. "J.P. Kellner's copy of Bach's sonatas and partitas for violin solo." *Early Music* 13 (1985): 199–211.

Very little has been written on the solo cello suites. An idiosyncratic reading of the set can be found in
Wilfrid Mellers. "Voice and body: Bach's solo cello suites as an apotheosis of the dance." In his *Bach and the dance of God,* 16–35. London, 1980.

For a survey of the lute works, see
Hans Neemann. "J.S. Bachs Lautenkompositionen." *BJ* 28 (1931): 72–87.

Concerning the works' intabulation and whether Bach was a lute player, see
Hans Radke. "War Johann Sebastian Bach Lautenspieler?" In *Festschrift Hans Engel zum siebzigsten Geburtstag,* edited by Horst Heussner, 281–89. Cassel, 1964.

Hans-Joachim Schulze. "Wer intavolierte Johann Sebastian Bachs Lautenkompositionen?" *Die Musikforschung* 19 (1966): 32–39.

On the style and dating of the solo flute partita, see
Robert L. Marshall. "J.S. Bach's compositions for solo flute: a reconsideration of their authenticity and chronology." *Journal of the American Musicological Society* 32 (1979): 463–98. Rev. in Marshall, *The music of Johann Sebastian Bach: the sources, the style, the significance,* 201–25. New York, 1989.

For some important new information on its dating, see
Yoshitake Kobayashi. "Noch einmal zu J.S. Bachs Solo pour la flute traversiere, BWV 1013." *Tibia* 16 (1990): 379–82.

8.2.4 Concertos

A useful literature survey is
Pippa Drummond. *The German concerto: five eighteenth-century studies,* 1–90. Oxford, 1980.

Various aspects of the repertory are discussed in more recent essays in

Peter Ahnsehl, Karl Heller and Hans-Joachim Schulze, eds. *Beiträge zum Konzertschaffen Johann Sebastian Bachs.* Bach-Studien 6. Leipzig, 1981.

Martin Geck and Werner Breig, eds. *Bachs Orchesterwerke: Bericht über das 1. Dortmunder Bach-Symposion im Januar 1996.* Dortmund, forthcoming.

The most important studies on chronology are

Hans-Joachim Schulze. "Johann Sebastian Bachs Konzerte—Fragen der Überlieferung und Chronologie." In *Beiträge zum Konzertschaffen Johann Sebastian Bachs,* edited by Peter Ahnsehl, Karl Heller and Hans-Joachim Schulze, 9–26. Bach-Studien 6. Leipzig, 1981.

Werner Breig. "Zur Chronologie von Johann Sebastian Bachs Konzertschaffen: Versuch eines neuen Zugangs." *Archiv für Musikwissenschaft* 40 (1983): 77–101.

The *Brandenburg Concertos* have generated a large body of literature, including many surveys. The best overview is

Malcolm Boyd. *Bach: the Brandenburg Concertos.* Cambridge, 1993.

For further interpretive work, see

Michael Marissen. *The social and religious designs of J.S. Bach's Brandenburg Concertos.* Princeton, 1995.

Study of the harpsichord concertos has focused on compositional process. The principal study is

Werner Breig. "Zum Kompositionsprozeß in Bachs Cembalokonzerten." In *Johann Sebastian Bachs Spätwerk und dessen Umfeld—Perspektiven und Probleme,* edited by Christoph Wolff, 32–47. Cassel, 1988.

On the forward-looking nature of this repertory, see also

Christian Berger. "J.S. Bachs Cembalokonzerte: ein Beitrag zur Gattungsgeschichte des Klavierkonzerts im 18. Jahrhundert." *Archiv für Musikwissenschaft* 47 (1990): 207–16.

Comparatively little has been written about the violin concertos. See

Martin Geck and Werner Breig, eds. *Bachs Orchesterwerke: Bericht über das 1. Dortmunder Bach-Symposion im Januar 1996.* Dortmund, forthcoming.

There has been much discussion on the origins and authorship of the Triple Concerto (BWV 1044), touching on a host of other issues as well. The most important studies are

Hans Eppstein. "Zur Vor- und Entstehungsgeschichte von J.S. Bachs Tripelkonzert a-Moll (BWV 1044)." In *Jahrbuch des Staatlichen Instituts für Musikforschung Preußischer Kulturbesitz, 1970*, 34–44. Berlin, 1971.

Peter Wollny. "Überlegungen zum Tripelkonzert a-Moll (BWV 1044)." In *Bachs Orchesterwerke: Bericht über das 1. Dortmunder Bach-Symposion im Januar 1996*, edited by Martin Geck and Werner Breig. Dortmund, forthcoming.

8.2.5 Suites

Comparatively little has been written about this repertory. Various aspects are covered by the essays in

Martin Geck and Werner Breig, eds. *Bachs Orchesterwerke: Bericht über das 1. Dortmunder Bach-Symposion im Januar 1996*. Dortmund, forthcoming.

8.2.6 Sonatas

A performer's survey of the repertory is provided by

Hans Vogt. *Johann Sebastian Bachs Kammermusik: Voraussetzungen, Analysen, Einzelwerke*. Stuttgart, 1981. Translated by Kenn Johnson as *Johann Sebastian Bach's chamber music: background, analyses, individual works*. Portland, 1988.

For an important overview of the pieces with obbligato harpsichord, see

Hans Eppstein. *Studien über J.S. Bachs Sonaten für ein Melodieinstrument und obligates Cembalo*. Uppsala, 1966.

Concerning the works with flute, see

Robert L. Marshall. "J.S. Bach's compositions for solo flute: a reconsideration of their authenticity and chronology." *Journal of the American Musicological Society* 32 (1979): 463–98. Rev. in his *The music of Johann Sebastian Bach: the sources, the style, the significance*, 201–25. New York, 1989.

For more on the continual debate over the authorship of the Sonata in E-flat BWV 1031, see

Jeanne Swack. "Quantz and the Sonata in E-flat major for flute and cembalo, BWV 1031." *Early Music* 23 (1995): 31–53.

For close critical readings of the works for viola da gamba, see

Laurence Dreyfus. "J.S. Bach and the status of genre: problems of style in the G-minor sonata BWV 1029." *Journal of Musicology* 5 (1987): 55–78. Rev. as "The status of a genre." In his *Bach and the patterns of invention,* 103–33. Cambridge, Mass., 1996.

Laurence Dreyfus. "Bachian invention and its mechanisms." In *The Cambridge companion to Bach,* edited by John Butt, 171–92. Cambridge, 1997.

8.2.7 *Canons,* Musical Offering, Art of Fugue

A survey of Bach's individually transmitted canons, which also considers their significance for Bach interpretation in general, is

Eric Chafe. "Allegorical music: the 'symbolism' of tonal language in the Bach canons." *Journal of Musicology* 3 (1984): 340–62.

On their dedicatees, see

Hans-Joachim Schulze. "Johann Sebastian Bachs Kanonwidmungen." *BJ* 53 (1967): 82–92.

There is an enormous literature on the *Musical Offering.* The classic studies are

Hans Theodore David. *J.S. Bach's Musical Offering: history, interpretation, and analysis.* New York, 1945.

Christoph Wolff. "New research on Bach's *Musical Offering.*" *Musical Quarterly* 57 (1971): 379–408. Rev. in his *Bach: essays on his life and music,* 239–58. Cambridge, Mass., 1991.

Work on questions of meaning and on the disposition of the original edition can also be found in

Ursula Kirkendale. "The source for Bach's *Musical Offering:* the *Institutio oratoria* of Quintilian." *Journal of the American Musicological Society* 33 (1980): 88–141. Rev. as "Bach und Quintilian: die *Institutio oratoria* als Modell des *Musikalischen Opfers.*" In *Musik in Antike und Neuzeit,* edited by Michael von Albrecht and Werner Schubert, 85–107. Frankfurt, 1987.

Michael Marissen. "More source-critical research on Bach's *Musical Offering*." *Bach* 25, no. 1 (1994): 11–27.

Michael Marissen. "The theological character of J.S. Bach's *Musical Offering*." In *Bach studies 2*, edited by Daniel R. Melamed, 85–106. Cambridge, 1995.

See also

Warren Kirkendale. "Ciceronians versus Aristotelians on the ricercar as exordium, from Bembo to Bach." *Journal of the American Musicological Society* 32 (1979): 1–44.

Paul Walker. "Rhetoric, the ricercar, and J.S. Bach's *Musical Offering*." In *Bach studies 2*, edited by Daniel R. Melamed, 175–91. Cambridge, 1995.

There is, likewise, an enormous literature on the *Art of Fugue*. Three recent and useful critical surveys are

Walter Kolneder. *Die Kunst der Fuge: Mythen des 20. Jahrhunderts*. 5 vols. Wilhelmshaven, 1977.

Peter Schleuning. *Johann Sebastian Bachs "Kunst der Fuge": Ideologien, Entstehung, Analyse*. Munich and Cassel, 1993.

Pieter Dirksen. *Studien zur Kunst der Fuge von Johann Sebastian Bach: Untersuchungen zur Entstehungsgeschichte, Struktur und Aufführungspraxis*. Wilhelmshaven, 1994.

Classic older studies that are still useful:

Wolfgang Graeser. "Bachs 'Kunst der Fuge.'" *BJ* 21 (1924): 1–104.

Donald Francis Tovey. *A companion to "The Art of Fugue" (Die Kunst der Fuge) J.S. Bach*. London, 1931, and reprints.

For important source-critical work sorting out problems of chronology and the completeness of the fugue BWV 1080/19, see

Christoph Wolff. "Zur Chronologie und Kompositionsgeschichte von Bachs Kunst der Fuge." *Beiträge zur Musikwissenschaft* 25 (1983): 130–42. Revised version translated by Alfred Mann as "The compositional history of the Art of Fugue." In Wolff, *Bach: essays on his life and music*, 265–81. Cambridge, Mass., 1991.

Christoph Wolff. "The last fugue: unfinished?" *Current Musicology* 19 (1975): 71–77. Rev. in his *Bach: essays on his life and music*, 259–64. Cambridge, Mass., 1991.

Work on the question of the disposition of the original edition is also found in

> Gregory Butler. "Ordering problems in J.S. Bach's *Art of Fugue* resolved." *Musical Quarterly* 69 (1983): 44–61.

For a spiritual-philosophical reading, see

> Hans Heinrich Eggebrecht. *Bachs Kunst der Fuge: Erscheinung und Deutung.* Munich, 1984. Translated by Jeffrey L. Prater as *J.S. Bach's* The Art of Fugue: *the work and its interpretation.* Ames, 1993.

The collection is often considered an ensemble work, but there are strong arguments favoring its conception for keyboard; while this point had been made by several authors, the most detailed and influential arguments were put forward by

> Gustav M. Leonhardt. *The Art of Fugue: Bach's last harpsichord work; an argument.* The Hague, 1952.

9

Bach's music in performance

Apart from organ and harpsichord playing, historically informed performance of Bach's music on instruments of his day or on replicas first started broadly to reach professional quality in the 1950s. Such performances have often dramatically changed modern perception of the repertories.

Of the *Bach-Jahrbuch* compilations mentioned in *1.2 Bibliographies,* each that was published since 1950 features extensive special listings entitled *Aufführungspraxis* (performance practice). Another useful bibliographic source on performance practice in general and Bach in particular (at pp. 263–90) is

> **Roland Jackson.** *Performance practice, medieval to contemporary: a bibliographic guide.* **New York, 1988.**

Supplements appear annually in the journal
> *Performance Practice Review.*

In this chapter, we will concentrate mainly on issues that have generated the most discussion and that have either influenced virtually all Bach performance or have significantly affected scholarship in other areas of Bach research (for example, chronology, editions).

> For a historical survey of styles of Bach performance, see
> **George B. Stauffer. "Changing issues of performance practice." In** *The Cambridge companion to Bach,* **edited by John Butt, 203–17. Cambridge, 1997.**

9.1 Vocal forces

The standard assumption in the scholarly literature, namely that Bach normally had choirs of approximately twelve voices reading from four vocal parts, was argued in
> **Arnold Schering. "Die Besetzung Bachscher Chöre."** *BJ* 17 (1920): 77–89.

Joshua Rifkin argues that Bach reckoned with an ensemble of four singers reading from four vocal parts, and several writers have entered into ardent debate with him; see

Joshua Rifkin. "Bach's chorus: a preliminary report." *Musical Times* 123 (1982): 747–54. Revised version as "Bachs Chor—ein vorläufiger Bericht." *Basler Jahrbuch für historische Musikpraxis* 9 (1985): 141–55.

Robert L. Marshall. "Bach's chorus: a preliminary reply to Joshua Rifkin." *Musical Times* 124 (1983): 19–22.

Joshua Rifkin. "Bach's chorus: a response to Robert Marshall." *Musical Times* 124 (1983): 161–62.

Joshua Rifkin. "Bach's chorus: some red herrings." *Journal of Musicological Research* 14 (1995): 223–34.

George Stauffer. "Response to Rifkin, 'Bach's chorus.'" *Journal of Musicological Research* 14 (1995): 234.

(Rifkin's "Some red herrings" essay is a response to criticism of the one-on-a-part Bach chorus in George Stauffer's review of John Butt, *Bach: Mass in B minor* [Cambridge, 1991] and Meredith Little and Natalie Jenne, *Dance and the music of J.S. Bach* [Bloomington, 1991] in *Journal of Musicological Research* 13 [1993]: 257–72.)

See also

Günther Wagner. "Die Chorbesetzung bei J.S. Bach und ihre Vorgeschichte: Anmerkungen zur 'hinlänglichen' Besetzung im 17. und 18. Jahrhundert." *Archiv für Musikwissenschaft* 43 (1986): 278–304.

Hans-Joachim Schulze. *Bach stilgerecht Aufführen—Wunschbild und Wirklichkeit: einige aufführungspraktische Aspekte von Johann Sebastian Bachs Leipziger Kirchenmusik.* Wiesbaden, 1991.

Andrew Parrot. "Bach's chorus: a 'brief yet highly necessary' reappraisal." *Early Music* 24 (1996): 551–80.

9.2 Instrumental forces

Here, too, there has been considerable disagreement over the size of the ensembles Bach actually had or wished he had.

Arguments for larger orchestras are put forward in

Reinhard Goebel. "Fragen der instrumentalen Solo- und Ensemblepraxis Bachs." In *Johann Sebastian Bachs Spätwerk und dessen Umfeld—*

Perspektiven und Probleme, edited by Christoph Wolff, 84–94. Cassel, 1988.

Hans-Joachim Schulze. "Johann Sebastian Bach's orchestra: some unanswered questions." *Early Music* 17 (1989): 3–15.

Arguments for smaller orchestras are found in
Joshua Rifkin. "More (and less) on Bach's orchestra." *Performance Practice Review* 4 (1991): 5–13.

The notion that in Bach's orchestras there were typically 2 to 4 violins altogether, normally with each performer reading from his own part, is explored explicitly in
Joshua Rifkin. "The violins in Bach's St. John Passion." In *Critica musica: essays in honor of Paul Brainard,* edited by John Knowles, 307–32. Amsterdam, 1996.

On the size of Bach's continuo sections and their scorings, see
Laurence Dreyfus. *Bach's continuo group: players and practices in his vocal works.* Cambridge, Mass., 1987.

Joshua Rifkin. "Some questions of performance in J.S. Bach's *Trauerode.*" In *Bach studies 2,* edited by Daniel R. Melamed, 119–53. Cambridge, 1995.

9.3 Instruments

See also *9.5 Pitch.*

Information on eighteenth-century instruments can be found conveniently in
Stanley Sadie, ed. *The New Grove dictionary of musical instruments,* 3 vols. London, 1984.

The classic study of Bach's instruments and their usage—very much in need of updating—is
Charles Sanford Terry. *Bach's orchestra.* London, 1932.

For a general and more recent introduction, see
Jürgen Eppelsheim. "Die Instrumente." In *Johann Sebastian Bach: Zeit, Leben, Wirken,* edited by Barbara Schwendowius and Wolfgang Döm-

ling, 127–42. Cassel, 1976. Translated by Gaynor Nitz as "The Instruments." In *Johann Sebastian Bach: life, times, influence*, edited by Barbara Schwendowius and Wolfgang Dömling, 127–42. Cassel, 1977.

For a detailed study—a model for further work—of Bach's usage of selected instruments (violin, violino piccolo, viola, violetta, viola d'amore, viola da gamba, recorder, flauto piccolo, flute, oboe da caccia, taille, cornetto, trombone, and timpani), see

Ulrich Prinz. "Studien zum Instrumentarium Johann Sebastian Bachs mit besonderer Berücksichtigung der Kantaten." Ph.D. diss. University of Tübingen, 1979.

Another exemplary and wide-ranging study, with further information on Bach and the flute, is

Ardal Powell and David Lasocki. "Bach and the flute: the players, the instruments, the music." *Early Music* 23 (1995): 9–29.

On the "Bach Organ" and related matters, see

Peter Williams. *The organ music of J.S. Bach.* Vol. 3, 117–95. Cambridge, 1984.

George Stauffer and Ernest May, eds. *J.S. Bach as organist: his instruments, music, and performance practices*, 3–53. Bloomington, 1986.

Quentin Faulkner. "Jacob Adlung's *Musica mechanica organoedi* and the 'Bach organ.'" *Bach* 21, no. 1 (1990): 42–59.

Quentin Faulkner. "Die Registrierung der Orgelwerke J.S. Bachs." *BJ* 81 (1995): 7–30.

On the sorts of harpsichord Bach would have been familiar with, see

Sheridan Germann. "The Mietkes, the Margrave and Bach." In *Bach, Handel, Scarlatti: tercentenary essays*, edited by Peter Williams, 119–48. Cambridge, 1985.

Dieter Krickeberg. "Einige Cembalotypen aus dem Umkreis von Johann Sebastian Bach und die historisierende Aufführungspraxis." In *Alte Musik als ästhetische Gegenwart—Bach, Händel, Schütz: Bericht über den internationalen musikwissenschaftlichen Kongreß Stuttgart 1985*, edited by Dietrich Berke and Dorothee Hanemann, vol. 2, 440–44. Cassel, 1987.

On Bach's continuo instruments and the various implications of their usage by Bach, see

Laurence Dreyfus. *Bach's continuo group: players and practices in his vocal works.* Cambridge, Mass., 1987.

9.4 Ornamentation and execution

For a critical overview of the subject, giving attention to Bach as well, see
Peter Schleuning. "Verzierungsforschung und Aufführungspraxis: zum Verhältnis von Notation und Interpretation in der Musik des 18. Jahrhunderts." *Basler Jahrbuch für historische Musikpraxis* 3 (1979): 11–114.

The classic study on Bach's ornaments is
Walter Emery. *Bach's ornaments.* London, 1953, and reprints.

Unusually lively and wide-ranging discussions of notation and performance are provided in
Frederick Neumann. *Ornamentation in Baroque and post-Baroque music: with special emphasis on J.S. Bach.* Princeton, 1978.

Slurring patterns in Bach's own manuscripts and their implications for performance practice, style criticism, and compositional process are analyzed in
John Butt. *Bach interpretation: articulation marks in primary sources of J.S. Bach.* Cambridge, 1990.

Close study of the Bach manuscripts for what they reveal about issues of tempo and dynamics is provided by
Robert L. Marshall. "Tempo and dynamic indications in the Bach sources: a review of the terminology." In *Bach, Handel, Scarlatti: tercentenary essays,* edited by Peter Williams, 259–75. Cambridge, 1985. Rev. in Marshall, *The music of Johann Sebastian Bach: the sources, the style, the significance,* 255–69. New York, 1989.

9.5 Pitch

Students of Bach's music have continually been confused by Bach's practice, especially in his earlier works, of notating certain instrumental parts in his vocal music in different keys from each other and from the voice parts. (To make matters worse, scholarly editions do not always accurately reflect Bach's notation.) This is mostly a matter of low-pitched woodwinds matching high-pitched organs. Although the relationships between the instruments are not so difficult to sort out, questions of pitch standards (that is, precisely how high or low the entire ensemble sounded) can get thorny. Apart from the practical implications for performance, study of these issues can also help in tracing a work's history: certain sorts of pitch relationships can be associated with particular places Bach worked.

In Bach's pre-Weimar vocal works, woodwinds are notated a whole step higher than the rest of the ensemble, because there the woodwinds were tuned that much lower than the strings, organ, and voices. In his Weimar compositions, woodwinds are usually tuned a minor third lower than the other forces, but in a few instances (involving a single oboe) a whole step lower. In his Leipzig compositions, the woodwinds, strings and voices are notated at the same pitch, while the organ is notated a whole step lower. The higher pitches are called *Chorton* ("choir pitch") and the lower pitches *Kammerton* ("chamber pitch").

A convenient place to go for descriptions of how these *Chorton* and *Kammerton* relationships worked out in individual cases is

Alfred Dürr. *Studien über die frühen Kantaten Johann Sebastian Bachs.* 2d ed. Wiesbaden, 1977.

How brass instruments fit into all of this is especially complicated, because, for example, horns could not only be built in different sizes but also adjusted in pitch through the use of crooks; furthermore, the keys in which their parts were notated relative to the rest of the ensemble were not as consistent as for woodwinds. On this subject, see

Thomas G. MacCracken. "Die Verwendung der Blechblasinstrumente bei J.S. Bach unter besonderer Berücksichtigung der Tromba da tirarsi." *BJ* 70 (1984): 59–89.

Don L. Smithers. "Die Verwendung der Blechblasinstrumente bei J.S. Bach unter besonderer Berücksichtigung der Tromba da tirarsi: kritische Anmerkungen zum gleichnamigen Aufsatz von Thomas G. MacCracken." *BJ* 76 (1990): 37–51.

Thomas G. MacCracken. "Nochmals: die Verwendung der Blechblasinstrumente bei J.S. Bach: Erwiderung auf Don L. Smithers' 'Kritische Anmerkungen.'" *BJ* 78 (1992): 123–30.

Reine Dahlqvist. "Corno and corno da caccia: horn terminology, horn pitches, and high horn parts." *Basler Jahrbuch für historische Musikpraxis* 15 (1991): 35–80.

On the notation of the cornetto and trombone parts, see

Ulrich Prinz. "Studien zum Instrumentarium Johann Sebastian Bachs mit besonderer Berücksichtigung der Kantaten," 186–216. Ph.D. diss. University of Tübingen, 1979.

On the notation of the recorder parts, see

Michael Marissen. "Organological questions and their significance in J.S. Bach's Fourth Brandenburg Concerto." *Journal of the American Musical Instrument Society* 17 (1991): 5–52.

On the notation of the oboe parts, see

Bruce Haynes. "Questions of tonality in Bach's cantatas: the woodwind perspective." *Journal of the American Musical Instrument Society* 12 (1986): 40–67.

On the notation of the continuo parts, see

Laurence Dreyfus. *Bach's continuo group: players and practices in his vocal works.* Cambridge, Mass., 1987.

Once the relative pitches of the parts have been determined, there remains the question of their actual frequency. The classic study of pitch standards in Bach is

Arthur Mendel. "On the pitches in use in Bach's time." *Musical Quarterly* 41 (1955): 332–54, 466–80. Reprint with appended revisions in Alexander J. Ellis and Arthur Mendel. *Studies in the history of musical pitch,* 187–224, 226–38 [226–38 are "Annotations, corrections, and additions (1965) by Arthur Mendel" (revisions concerning the Bach essay at pp. 235–38)]. Amsterdam, 1968. Further updating in Mendel. "Pitch in Western music since 1500: a re-examination." *Acta musicologica* 50 (1978): 1–93, 328.

More recent research that comes persuasively to substantially different conclusions was published as

Bruce Haynes. "Johann Sebastian Bach's pitch standards: the woodwind perspective." *Journal of the American Musical Instrument Society* 11 (1985): 55–114.

See also

Bruce Haynes. "Pitch standards in the Baroque and Classical periods." Ph.D. diss. University of Montreal, 1995.

We offer here a summary of Mendel's and Haynes's conclusions. Both agree on the relative pitches of Bach's parts; at issue is their historical nomenclature and actual frequencies.

Haynes concluded that in Bach's day there were two levels of *Kammerton* (A at c.410 and c.390 Hz, the latter called *Tief-Kammerton*, or "French pitch") and two levels of *Chorton* (A at c.460 and c.490 Hz). He argued that Bach's *Chorton* was the lower variety.

Mendel had concluded that the *Chorton* A at Bach's regular venues was c.490 Hz and that there were two *Kammerton* levels, one a major second and the other a minor third lower than *Chorton*. Mendel took *B-Kammerton* to refer to the higher *Kammerton*, and *A-Kammerton* and *Tief-Kammerton* to be different names for the lower one, where A is c.410 Hz; Mendel also, however, understood "French pitch" to refer to A at c.390 Hz.

Haynes argued that *A-Kammerton* and *B-Kammerton* actually refer to an identical frequency, the different names having to do with this same level's relation to the two types of *Chorton;* that is, in relation to the higher *Chorton*, the *Kammerton* note C sounded like the *Chorton* note A, and in relation to the lower variety of *Chorton*, this same *Kammerton* note C sounded like a B-flat ("B" in German corresponds to B-flat in English, "H" to B-natural).

Thus, for example, for Haynes the voices and strings in the Leipzig church cantatas were oriented to a *Kammerton* A 410, for Mendel to a *Kammerton* A 440. Both views are internally logical, but Haynes had the advantage of new organological research: from much more extensive study of historical instruments, there appears to be practically no evidence of a *Kammerton* at A 440 in Bach's Germany, and furthermore, organs are overwhelmingly at A c.460.

For practical solutions to questions of tonality in Bach's cantatas, see
Bruce Haynes. "Questions of tonality in Bach's cantatas: the woodwind perspective." *Journal of the American Musical Instrument Society* **12 (1986): 40–67.**

10

Bach as composer

10.1 Compositional process

The principal study of Bach's working methods in his vocal compositions is
Robert L. Marshall. *The compositional process of J.S. Bach: a study of the
autograph scores of the vocal works.* **2 vols. Princeton, 1972.**

This study considers Bach's use of paper, the types of his handwriting, and
the stages of his conception and writing down of various kinds of movements; it includes a catalogue and transcription of sketches and drafts.

On questions of Bach's musical invention construed more broadly, see
Laurence Dreyfus. *Bach and the patterns of invention.* **Cambridge,
Mass., 1996.**

On the role of text in Bach's compositional process, see
**Paul Brainard. "The regulative and generative roles of verse in Bach's
'thematic' invention." In** *Bach studies,* **edited by Don O. Franklin, 54–
74. Cambridge, 1989.**

On Bach's transcriptions and arrangements, see
Ulrich Siegele. *Kompositionsweise und Bearbeitungstechnik in der Instrumentalmusik Johann Sebastian Bachs.* **Neuhausen-Stuttgart, 1975.**

On Bach's parody technique, see *7.2.8 Parody.*

10.2 Bach and the music of other composers

For literature on Bach's contact with specific works of other composers, see
4.2 Bach's library, especially the references in the entry for each work in
Kirsten Beißwenger. *Johann Sebastian Bachs Notenbibliothek.* **Cassel,
1992.**

On Bach's contact with musical repertories, see:

Seventeenth-century music in general

Christoph Wolff. "Bach and the legacy of the seventeenth century." In *Bach studies 2*, edited by Daniel R. Melamed, 192–201. Cambridge, 1995.

Stephen A. Crist. "The early works and the heritage of the seventeenth century." In *The Cambridge companion to Bach*, edited by John Butt, 75–85. Cambridge, 1997.

French music

Hans-Joachim Schulze. "The French influence in Bach's instrumental music." *Early Music* 13 (1985): 180–84.

George B. Stauffer. "Boyvin, Grigny, D'Anglebert, and Bach's assimilation of French Classical organ music." *Early Music* 21 (1993): 83–96.

Early keyboard repertory

Robert Stephen Hill. "The Möller Manuscript and the Andreas Bach Book: two keyboard anthologies from the circle of the young Johann Sebastian Bach." Ph.D. diss. Harvard University, 1987.

Robert Hill, ed. *Keyboard music from the Andreas Bach Book and the Möller Manuscript*. Cambridge, Mass., 1991.

Palestrina-style counterpoint

Christoph Wolff. *Der Stile antico in der Musik Johann Sebastian Bachs: Studien zu Bachs Spätwerk*. Wiesbaden, 1968.

Music by the Bach family (Altbachisches Archiv) / German motets

Daniel R. Melamed. *J.S. Bach and the German motet*. Cambridge, 1995.

On Bach and selected other composers, see:

Johann Ludwig Bach

Johann Ludwig was J.S. Bach's cousin, active mostly at the court of Meiningen. J.S. Bach performed at least 18 of his church cantatas at the end of his second year in Leipzig.

William H. Scheide. "Johann Sebastian Bachs Sammlung von Kantaten seines Vetters Johann Ludwig Bach." *BJ* 46 (1959): 52–94; 48 (1961): 5–24; 49 (1962): 5–32.

Georg Böhm

Jean-Claude Zehnder. "Georg Böhm und Johann Sebastian Bach: zur Chronologie der Bachschen Stilentwicklung." *BJ* 74 (1988): 73–110.

Dietrich Buxtehude

Christoph Wolff. "Dietrich Buxtehude and seventeenth-century music in retrospect." In *Church, stage, and studio: music and its contexts in seventeenth-century Germany,* edited by Paul Walker, 3–20. Ann Arbor, 1990. Also as "Buxtehude, Bach, and seventeenth-century music in retrospect." In Wolff, *Bach: essays on his life and music,* 41–55. Cambridge, Mass., 1991.

Johann Joseph Fux

Johann Trummer and Rudolf Flotzinger, eds. *Johann Sebastian Bach und Johann Joseph Fux: Bericht über das Symposion anläßlich des 58. Bachfestes der Neuen Bachgesellschaft 24.–29. Mai 1983 in Graz.* Cassel, 1985.

Johann Adam Reinken

Christoph Wolff. "Johann Adam Reinken und Johann Sebastian Bach: zum Kontext des Bachschen Frühwerks." *BJ* 71 (1985): 99–118. Translated as "Johann Adam Reinken and Johann Sebastian Bach: on the context of Bach's early works." In *J.S. Bach as organist: his instruments, music, and performance practices,* edited by George Stauffer and Ernest May, 57–80. Bloomington, 1986. Also as "Bach and Johann Adam Reinken: a context for the early works." In Wolff, *Bach: essays on his life and music,* 56–71. Cambridge, Mass., 1991.

Antonio Vivaldi

On documentary and source-critical aspects of Bach's contact with Vivaldi's music, see
Hans-Joachim Schulze. *Studien zur Bach-Überlieferung im 18. Jahrhundert,* 146–73. Leipzig, 1984.

On musical aspects, see
Christoph Wolff. "Vivaldi's compositional art and the process of 'musical thinking.'" In *Nuovi Studi Vivaldiani,* vol. 1, edited by Antonio Fanna and Giovanni Morelli, 1–17. Florence, 1988. Rev. as "Vivaldi's compositional art, Bach, and the process of 'musical think-

ing.'" In Wolff, *Bach: essays on his life and music,* 72–83. Cambridge, Mass., 1991.

10.3 Dance

For a survey of eighteenth-century dance types and their appearance primarily in Bach's instrumental music, see

Meredith Little and Natalie Jenne. *Dance and the music of J.S. Bach.* **Bloomington, 1991.**

On dance types as they appear in Bach's vocal music, see

Doris Finke-Hecklinger. *Tanzcharaktere in Johann Sebastian Bachs Vokalmusik.* **Tübinger Bach-Studien 6. Trossingen, 1970.**

11

Approaches to Bach's music

11.1 Tone-painting

The classic studies on tone-painting in Bach (the notion that certain motivic shapes have nearly "verbal" significance) are

Albert Schweitzer. *J.S. Bach, le musicien-poète.* Leipzig, 1905. Exp. version in German as *J.S. Bach.* Leipzig, 1908, and reprints. Latter translated by Ernest Newman, with minor additions by the author, as *J.S. Bach.* Leipzig and New York, 1911, and reprints.

André Pirro. *L'Esthétique de Jean-Sébastien Bach.* Paris, 1907.

Manfred Bukofzer. "Allegory in Baroque music." *Journal of the Warburg and Courtauld Institutes* 3 (1939–40): 1–21.

11.2 Theological studies

Good introductions to theological Bach interpretation are

Renate Steiger. "Methode und Ziel einer musikalischen Hermeneutik im Werke Bachs." *Musik und Kirche* 47 (1977): 209–24.

Robin A. Leaver. *J.S. Bach as preacher: his Passions and music in worship.* St. Louis, 1984.

Robin A. Leaver. "Music and Lutheranism" and "The mature vocal works and their theological and liturgical context." In *The Cambridge companion to Bach,* edited by John Butt, 35–45 and 86–122. Cambridge, 1997.

For a survey of the field, see

Walter Blankenburg. "Theologische Bachforschung heute." *Augsburger Jahrbuch für Musikwissenschaft* 2 (1985): 91–106.

Most theological study of Bach has focused mainly on the librettos of the vocal works, not so much on the notes or how the words and notes together generate religious meanings. See, for example:

Martin Petzoldt, ed. *Bach als Ausleger der Bibel: theologische und musikwissenschaftliche Studien zum Werk Johann Sebastian Bachs.* Göttingen, 1985.

Jaroslav Pelikan. *Bach among the theologians.* Philadelphia, 1986.

For studies that feature closer theological engagement with the music itself, see

Friedrich Smend. *Johann Sebastian Bach—Kirchenkantaten.* 3d ed. Berlin, 1966.

Friedrich Smend. *Bach-Studien: gesammelte Reden und Aufsätze,* edited by Christoph Wolff. Cassel, 1969.

Eric Chafe. *Tonal allegory in the vocal music of J.S. Bach.* Berkeley, 1991.

Chafe's book may seem particularly difficult for some beginning students; a layperson's introduction was published as

Eric Chafe. "Luther's 'analogy of faith' in Bach's church music." *dialog* 24 (1985): 96–101.

For examples of close theological readings of individual instrumental works, see

Ulrich Siegele. *Bachs theologischer Formbegriff und das Duett F-Dur: ein Vortrag.* Neuhausen-Stuttgart, 1978. Translated as "Bach's theological concept of form and the F Major Duet." *Music Analysis* 11 (1992): 245–78.

Michael Marissen. "The theological character of J.S. Bach's *Musical Offering.*" In *Bach studies 2,* edited by Daniel R. Melamed, 85–106. Cambridge, 1995.

Concerning issues of Bach and antisemitism, see

Dagmar Hoffmann-Axthelm. "Bach und die *perfidia Iudaica:* zur Symmetrie der Juden-Turbae in der Johannes-Passion." *Basler Jahrbuch für historische Musikpraxis* 13 (1989): 31–54.

Michael Marissen. *Lutheranism, anti-Judaism, and Bach's St. John Passion.* New York, 1998.

11.3 Bach's music and society

Much has been written to give students a good sense of the social *background* to Bach (see *3. Bach's life*), but scholarship has for the most part not focused so closely on how the form and content of Bach's music itself might reflect or promote social ideas.

For a stimulating and controversial introduction to the subject, see
Susan McClary. "The blasphemy of talking politics during Bach year." In *Music and society: the politics of composition, performance and reception,* edited by Richard Leppert and Susan McClary, 13–62. Cambridge, 1987.

For an approach that is more historically grounded and that reaches both similar and contrasting conclusions, see
Michael Marissen. *The social and religious designs of J.S. Bach's Brandenburg Concertos.* Princeton, 1995.

Social interpretation of the structural proportions in Bach's music has been explored in
Ulrich Siegele. "Schöpfungs- und Gesellschaftsordnung in Bachs Musik." In *Im Gespräch: der Mensch—ein interdisziplinärer Dialog; Joseph Möller zum 65. Geburtstag,* edited by Heribert Gauly et al., 276–85. Düsseldorf, 1981.

For examples of close social readings of individual works, see
Erich Reimer. "Bachs Jagdkantate als profanes Ritual: zur politischen Funktion absolutistischer Hofmusik." *Musik und Bildung* 12 (1971): 674–83.

Irving Godt. "Politics, patriotism, and a polonaise: a possible revision in Bach's *Suite in B Minor." Musical Quarterly* 74 (1990): 610–22.

11.4 Reception

Some branches of interpretation have sought grounding in the historical traditions of how their topics have been understood, the idea being that whatever commonality emerges probably reflects something essential about the subject's meanings.

For an introduction to the subject, see

Martin Zenck. "Bach reception: some concepts and parameters." In *The Cambridge companion to Bach,* edited by John Butt, 218–25. Cambridge, 1997.

On early Bach reception, see

Gerhard Herz. *Johann Sebastian Bach im Zeitalter des Rationalismus und der Frühromantik.* Cassel, 1935. Translated by Herz as "Johann Sebastian Bach in the age of rationalism and early romanticism." In his *Essays on J.S. Bach,* xv–xxxi, 1–124. Ann Arbor, 1985.

Martin Zenck. "Stadien der Bach-Deutung in der Musikkritik, Musikästhetik und Musikgeschichtsschreibung zwischen 1750 und 1800." *BJ* 68 (1982): 7–32.

Hans-Joachim Schulze. "'Unbequemes Geräusche' und 'gelehrte Chaos': Bemerkungen zur Bach-Rezeption im 18. und frühen 19. Jahrhundert." In *Alte Musik als ästhetische Gegenwart—Bach, Händel, Schütz: Bericht über den internationalen musikwissenschaftlichen Kongreß Stuttgart 1985,* edited by Dietrich Berke and Dorothee Hanemann, vol. 1, 137–43. Cassel, 1987.

Ludwig Finscher. "Bach in the eighteenth century." In *Bach studies,* edited by Don O. Franklin, 281–96. Cambridge, 1989.

Martin Zenck. "Bach in der Musikgeschichtsschreibung und in der Musik des 18. Jahrhunderts." *Jahrbuch des Staatlichen Instituts für Musikforschung Preußischer Kulturbesitz, 1985/86,* 239–56. Cassel, 1989.

A much-investigated problem in early Bach reception concerns a dispute between Bach's student Johann Adolph Scheibe and Bach's friend Johann Abraham Birnbaum over the nature of Bach's music. See

George J. Buelow. "In defense of J.A. Scheibe against J.S. Bach." *Proceedings of the Royal Musical Association* 101 (1974/75): 85–100.

Günther Wagner. "J.A. Scheibe—J.S. Bach: Versuch einer Bewertung." *BJ* 68 (1982): 33–49.

On the nineteenth century, see also

Martin Geck. *Die Wiederentdeckung der Matthäuspassion im 19. Jahrhundert: die zeitgenössischen Dokumente und ihre ideengeschichtliche Deutung.* Regensburg, 1967.

Martin Zenck. *Die Bach-Rezeption des späten Beethoven: zum Verhältnis von Musikhistoriographie und Rezeptionsgeschichtsschreibung der "Klassik."* Stuttgart, 1986.

On the twentieth century, see

Martin Zenck. "Wenn Bach Bienen gezüchtet hätte." In *Bach im 20. Jahrhundert: 59. Bachfest der Neuen Bachgesellschaft in Verbindung mit Kasseler Musiktage / Neue Musik in der Kirche,* 102–26. Cassel, 1984.

For studies on individual composers of the nineteenth and twentieth centuries and their reception of Bach, see

Ingrid Fuchs and Susanne Antonicek, eds. *Johann Sebastian Bach: Beiträge zur Wirkungsgeschichte.* Vienna, 1992.

Martin Zenck. "Reinterpreting Bach in the nineteenth and twentieth centuries." In *The Cambridge companion to Bach,* edited by John Butt, 226–50. Cambridge, 1997.

Michael Marissen, ed. *Creative responses to Bach from Mozart to Hindemith.* Bach perspectives 3. Lincoln, 1998.

Concerning Bach and the notion of "absolute music," see also

Carl Dahlhaus. "Bach-Rezeption und ästhetische Autonomie." In *Alte Musik als ästhetische Gegenwart—Bach, Händel, Schütz: Bericht über den internationalen musikwissenschaftlichen Kongreß Stuttgart 1985,* edited by Dietrich Berke and Dorothee Hanemann, vol. 1, 18–26. Cassel, 1987.

11.5 Numerology

An enormous amount has been written about number symbolism and Bach. We are concerned here not so much with the relatively uncontroversial, more straightforward sort, where Bach might call attention to the number 3 to refer to the Trinity, 10 to the Ten Commandments, and so on, but rather with the assigning of numerical values to letters of the alphabet and "demonstrating" that the numbers of notes or measures spell out certain significant words. Advanced scholarship, for the most part, has not taken these claims seriously, but they have generated much activity.

A full survey of the issues is

Ruth Tatlow. *Bach and the riddle of the number alphabet.* Cambridge, 1991.

This is essential reading, as it exposes problems in the fundamental premises of the theory: Number alphabets used in Bach's day and earlier never assigned 1 to A, 2 to B, 3 to C, and so on. Furthermore, number alphabets were used not for musical purposes but to interpret scripture (for example, in mystical Judaism), and interpreting scripture in this way was severely frowned upon in Lutheranism.

In Bach interpretation, the approach started with
Friedrich Smend. *Johann Sebastian Bach—Kirchenkantaten,* vol. 3, 5–21. **Berlin, 1947.**

The first major challenge to Smend's work on historical grounds was provided by
Ulrich Meyer. "Zahlenalphabet bei J.S. Bach? Zur antikabbalistischen Tradition im Luthertum." *Musik und Kirche* 51 **(1981): 15–19.**

11.6 Analysis

Bach's music has figured in analytical and theoretical writings of all kinds since the eighteenth century. There is a particularly extensive literature on the *Well-Tempered Clavier,* the *Art of Fugue* and the four-part chorales. Analyses of individual works by Bach are cited in the tools discussed in *1. Bibliographic tools of Bach research;* note especially the heading "Analysis" in the *Bach Compendium*'s bibliographies. Here we cite only a few items that focus on Bach's music by especially influential writers.

Hugo Riemann's principal writing on fugue concentrates on Bach's music:
Hugo Riemann. *Katechismus der Fugen-Komposition (Analyse von J.S. Bachs "Wohltemperiertem Klavier" und "Kunst der Fuge").* 3 vols. **Leipzig, 1890–94. Vols. 1–2 translated by J.S. Shedlock as** *Analysis of J.S. Bach's Wohltemperirtes* [sic] *Clavier (48 preludes & fugues).* **London, n.d.**

Ernst Kurth's influential treatise on melody and the roles of "kinetic energy," the unconscious, and musical sound takes Bach's music as its subject:
Ernst Kurth. *Grundlagen des linearen Kontrapunkts: Bachs melodische Polyphonie.* **3d ed. Bern, 1922.**

These issues and their historical significance are discussed in
Carl Dahlhaus. "Bach und der 'lineare Kontrapunkt.'" *BJ* 49 **(1962): 58–79.**

Bach's music figured prominently in the writings of Heinrich Schenker. Bach analyses appear in his pathbreaking yearbook *Das Meisterwerk in der Musik:*

Heinrich Schenker. *Das Meisterwerk in der Musik,* vol. 2, 97–104. Munich, 1926. Translated by Hedi Siegel as "The sarabande of J.S. Bach's suite no. 3 for unaccompanied violoncello (BWV 1009)." *Music Forum* 2 (1970): 274–82.

Heinrich Schenker. *Das Meisterwerk in der Musik,* vol. 1, 61–73. Munich, 1926. Translated by John Ratgeb as "The largo of J.S. Bach's sonata no. 3 for unaccompanied violin (BWV 1005)." *Music Forum* 4 (1976): 141–59.

Two Bach analyses also appear in

Heinrich Schenker. *Fünf Urlinie-Tafeln / Five analyses in sketchform.* New York, [1933]. Reprinted as *Five graphic music analyses (Fünf Urlinie-Tafeln): with a new introduction and glossary by Felix Salzer.* New York, 1969.

On Schenker and Bach see also

Walter Kolneder. "Sind Schenkers Analysen Beiträge zur Bacherkenntnis?" *Deutsches Jahrbuch der Musikwissenschaft* 3 (1958): 59–73.

Index of Names

Index of titles

This index is alphabetized strictly letter by letter, ignoring all spaces, punctuation, and initial articles. Thus, *Bach's ornaments* is followed by *Bach sources in America*.

Index of Subjects

absolute music, 154
accompanied recitatives. *See* recitatives
Altbachisches Archiv, 25, 147
Amalienbibliothek, 66, 74
America, Bach sources in, 80
American Bach Society, 10, 13, 20
Andreas Bach Book, 25, 147
Anhalt-Köthen. *See* Köthen
Anhang (BWV), 4–5
antisemitism, 151
arias, 109
ariosos, 110
Arnstadt, 39
Aufklärung. *See* Enlightenment
Augsburg, 52
Austrian National Library. *See* Vienna,
   Österreichische Nationalbibliothek

Bach-Archiv (Leipzig), 10, 37, 79, 89, 92
Bach family, 24–27, 30, 38–39, 48, 50–51,
   65–67, 71–73, 147
"Bachische Auction," 54, 73
Bach, Johann Sebastian
   ancestors, 24–25. *See also* Bach family
   Bible, 34–36, 53
   biographies, 31–37
   children, 26–27, 29–30, 51
   chronology, 37
   compositional process, 106, 112, 123,
      125, 133, 142, 146
   estate, 71–72
   heirs, 72–73
   iconography, 30–31
   image, 34–37
   library, 15, 53–54, 71–72, 101
   obituary, 27, 31–32, 112, 116–17, 119
   portraits. *See* iconography
   as progressive, 35–36, 46
   students, 50–52
   teaching, 49–50, 124

   wives, 25
Bach, J.S.: works—general
   analysis, 155–56
   arrangements, 129, 146
   authenticity, 4–5, 89, 124–25, 132, 134
   chronology, 3–4, 16, 41, 64–66, 68, 72,
      107–08, 112–13, 115, 124, 128–34,
      136
   dance, 16, 112, 132, 139, 149
   early works, 13, 19, 25, 41, 64, 66, 107–
      08, 115, 128, 130, 143, 147–48
   editions, 82–101
   intabulation, 132
   late works, 19, 64, 108–09, 147
   librettists, 104–05
   melodic index, 81
   numerology, 154–55
   parody, 15, 111, 117, 119–20, 122–23
   reception, 152–54
   and society, 152
   stile antico, 109, 147
   text, vocal, 102–04
   thematic catalogues, 3–7
   thematic index, 81
   tonal allegory, 112, 120–21, 151
   tonal ordering, 129
   tone-painting, 150
   transcriptions, 146
   translations (vocal texts), 104, 125
   worklists, 81
Bach, J.S.: works—instrumental
   canons, 135
   cello works, 131–32, 156
   chamber music, 129, 131, 134
   chorale preludes, 128, 130
   concerto arrangements, 40, 146
   concertos, 5, 14, 47, 127, 132–34, 144,
      152
   flute works, 131–32, 134–35, 141
   fugues, 13, 108, 128, 130, 135–37, 155

Index of Bach's works

This index excludes works listed in the tables of the liturgy, BG, and NBA. For works in various genres, consult the table of contents.